BUILT ON SOLID PRINCIPLES
The Melaleuca Story

BUILT ON SOLID PRINCIPLES

the Melaleuca Story

by RICHARD M. BARRY

Published by
RM Barry Publications
P.O. Box 3528
Littleton, CO 80161-3528

1 (888) 209-0510
Fax (303) 224-0299

ISBN 0-9665924-0-9

Printed in the United States of America
Cover photograph copyright © 1997 PhotoDisc, Inc.

Please note: In this book, it should be understood that the term "melaleuca oil" is a general term referring to the oil distilled from the leaves of the Melaleuca alternifolia tree. When referring to the specific product sold by Melaleuca, Inc., the trade name of "Melaleuca® oil" is used, including the ® symbol.

How to Order:

This book is available through RM Barry Publications. Quantity discounts are available. Please call toll-free for prices and order information, 1 (888) 209-0510. Or call to receive a catalog of our other publications.

Acknowledgements

This book would not exist if it had not been for the efforts of many dedicated people.

John Beaulieu, who tirelessly worked with me throughout this project, pouring through research and lending his invaluable insights every step of the way.

Tina Barry, my beautiful wife, who often gave her evening, after a long day with three demanding children, to critique the latest draft of each chapter.

Prem Pitts, the eminently capable writer who took my rough manuscript and turned it into a piece of work I could be proud of; and in the process, became a friend.

All of the Melaleuca leaders who contributed their ideas, insights, and encouragement. Your passion for enhancing lives and for the company is always inspiring to me.

And others who played a role in making this book possible, like **Lisa Beaulieu, Gordon Curry, Karen Garnett,** and **Tom McCrary**.

Table of Contents

Introduction

"Men make history, and not the other way around, ...
Progress occurs when courageous, skillful leaders
seize the opportunity to change things for the better."

—Harry S. Truman

 In 1985, an American businessman, the son of a humble Idaho railroad worker found himself in a position which is every business-man's personal nightmare. He had burned his bridges behind him, leaving a secure career and high-paying job for a venture that had turned out to be nothing more than a major lemon. His dilemma was particularly painful. Not only did he passionately want the venture to succeed, but he was possessed with a character trait not usually found in the dog-eat-dog world of business—he cared. He cared, not only about the integrity of the enterprise, but for all those his business touched.

The story has a happy ending.

The businessman analyzed the reasons for the venture's failure. From this, he constructed a model for a business that would not only succeed but would do so with grace. Drawing on the down-home values of his wholesome Idaho upbringing, he turned a lemon into lemonade. He even went further than that. He planted the seeds from the lemon and a giant tree flourished and produces fruit to this day.

That man is, of course, Frank VanderSloot, co-founder of Melaleuca, Inc.

At one level this may seem to be the onset of a rags-to-riches story and, indeed, there is a component of that. Frank VanderSloot was recently appointed to the Board of Directors of the United States Chamber of Commerce, the most powerful business force in the nation's capital. Furthermore, his home state of Idaho has bestowed upon him the title of Idaho's Business Leader of the Year.

It is a tale of lessons learned, of weaknesses transformed into strength and adversity into triumph.

However, this is more than the story of what Frank attained. Nor is it simply a description of what he built. Of paramount significance is *how* he built an organization of such solid integrity that it has survived the fickle economic climate of the 90's and has continued to flourish beyond all expectations.

It is a tale of lessons learned, of weaknesses transformed into strength and adversity into triumph. It is a model for all those who have ever had to deal with failure and the bitter experiences of promises unfilled.

Although there were three founding partners of Melaleuca, it is no disrespect to the merits of the other partners, Roger and Allen Ball, to say that Melaleuca, Inc. would not be what it is today without the vision of the president and CEO, Frank L. VanderSloot.

Frank founded Melaleuca, Inc. on the basis of a mission statement. This was not just rhetoric, but a powerful principle that is a key to the Melaleuca experience. "To enhance the lives of those we touch" is its aim. It is impossible to separate the mission statement from the man, the principle is so essential to Frank's being.

Thus, in order to convey the crucial role that Frank VanderSloot's values have played in the forming of Melaleuca, each chapter of this book is written around one of the founding principles.

In Chapter One, we learn about the discovery of melaleuca oil by the Ball brothers and the failure of Melaleuca, Inc.'s predecessor, Oil of Melaleuca, Inc. This failure was a turning point in Frank's life, enabling him to form a company based on personal values which he felt essential to the survival of a business. Thus, the new company, Melaleuca, Inc., was built on a structure which avoided all the pitfalls of the failed business and formed the foundations for a new style of business. This gives the chapter its title and its purpose—*"Building a Business to Last a Lifetime."*

Chapter Two presents the key elements in Frank's personal development. We meet his mentors, the men and women who enabled him to become what he is today, particularly his father and Peter Dalebout. With

In order to convey the crucial role that Frank VanderSloot's values have played in the forming of Melaleuca, each chapter of this book is written around one of the founding principles.

their input, Frank was empowered to slough off his personal limitations and to blossom into a powerful leader such that he has touched the lives of hundreds of thousands of people positively. Frank's transformation is an actual realization of the belief that one person can make a difference. It is a principle that Frank has called *"The Power of One."*

In Chapter Three, we discuss the innovative Consumer Direct Marketing™ system. The aim of this system is no less than to give all Americans an equal opportunity. This is not just an opportunity to earn more, but also to enjoy the freedom given by money—time. Time for family, love, friendships, relationships. Time for those things which VanderSloot sincerely believes are what life is all about. Key elements in the system are discussed in detail, as well as their implications and ramifications, revealing how Melaleuca's Marketing Executives can accomplish its goal of *"Redistributing the Opportunity for Wealth."*

One of the basic credos of Melaleuca is that no one should be hurt—either *in* the business or *by* the business. The latter is achieved by an emphasis on quality products made from natural substances which are beneficial to the customer and yet have minimal impact on the environment.

The aim of this system is no less than to give all Americans an equal opportunity.

By networking with the scientific community, Melaleuca has produced superlative products at competitive prices. As a result, Melaleuca has become an innovator in the fields of nutrition, health and household cleaning products—all designed to improve the quality of life. Melaleuca has evolved a system whereby they take the best from nature and use science to unlock its secrets and validate its benefits—in other words, *"The Best of Science and Nature."*

In the final chapter, we learn how this policy of networking with scientists to investigate new developments in natural products has led Melaleuca to an incredible pioneer product that, in the coming months, may revolutionize a billion-dollar industry and change forever the way Americans deal with the #1 killer in the U.S.—heart disease. *"What the Future Holds"* for Melaleuca is yet to be seen. But all indications are, the future looks very bright—very bright indeed.

At the root of this phenomenal success, the driving force is the mission statement—and no one speaks more eloquently about this than Frank VanderSloot himself ...

A videotaped interview in VanderSloot's office[1]
Frank VanderSloot sits in a comfortable armchair, relaxed. He is calm beneath the glare of the bright lights and answers the interviewer's questions with the proficiency of a man who knows his facts. It is Frank, the seasoned businessman who sits there so easily; the man who inspired sufficient confidence in the United States Chamber of Commerce that they singled him out "to be an outstanding member of the Board."[2]

The interview gains momentum. Frank answers without hesitation. He obviously knows his subject well. The interviewer asks about *"We're about helping people reach their values."* Melaleuca's mission statement. Frank reiterates it, a statement reproduced countless times in Melaleuca literature. When he says it, the words suddenly resonate with a quiet power. "To enhance the lives of those we touch by helping people reach their goals."

The statement rings with the intriguing freshness of a deeply-held conviction. He talks about the things that bring people joy; their values; the things that are really important—family, relationships. "We're about helping people reach *their* values," Frank insists.

The interviewer asks about the key to Melaleuca's success. A subtle change comes over Frank. He leans forward, his tone sharpens. "It's the products. Clearly it's the products." He is still calm but his voice is animated. "I feel that sometimes there's a tendency for people to present that it's the marketing plan that brings us our success." He looks pained. It is obvious this is a major concern. "Without having the best products that money can buy, we really don't have an excuse to be here."

The interviewer asks if there is anything that could stop the company's growth. "If we lost sight of who we are and what we stand for. If we lost sight of ethics." He shakes his head. "If somehow we let greed creep in ..."

The interviewer asks about Frank's vision for Melaleuca. "Well it's exciting. The world's wide open for us ..." Frank's face changes to a broad smile. "If we do it right ... we can capitalize on this $200 billion industry ... so, we've not even started."

As the lights dim and the interview ends, you are left with the distinct impression that this is not a public-relations stance by Frank VanderSloot. He is, in effect, living out values which he cannot, and will not, live without. That Melaleuca is not simply a business, but a cause.

He is, in effect, living out values which he cannot, and will not, live without. That Melaleuca is not simply a business, but a cause.

Because Melaleuca is more than just a business, because it has as its core belief those values of loyalty, friendship, family and freedom dear to all mankind, it has survived and it will survive. It has been built on principles as solid and enduring as stone. Therefore, any impression of Melaleuca is best presented by the granite background and stone pillars depicted on the cover of this book. If a builder were to construct a building with longevity as his primary objective, he would probably choose stone as his building material. Building a business to last a lifetime is one of Melaleuca's top objectives. And it *will* last a lifetime—and beyond. It will still be flourishing when its leaders have long gone. Frank VanderSloot made it that way because it is *"Built On Solid Principles."*

Sheltered by the sturdy edifice of these principles, there has flourished a gigantic tree whose branches protrude wider and whose roots dig deep even into the thin soil of the precarious 90's. The tree blossoms today and its fruit can be shared by anyone who wants to stand with Frank beneath those stout stone pillars.

This is the story you are about to read—the story of Melaleuca, Inc. It is not just Frank VanderSloot's story or my story—it is *our* story.

CHAPTER 1

Building a Business to Last a Lifetime

*"Real integrity stays in place whether
the test is adversity or prosperity."*

—Charles Swindoll

 Melaleuca, Inc. is now thirteen years into its phenomenal growth. As such, it would be difficult to sum up its success in a few words. Indeed, that is the purpose of this story. It is possible, though, to pinpoint some of the basic building blocks of its solid foundation. One key factor is quality products.

Whenever Frank VanderSloot is praised for the superior nature of his marketing plan, he is quick to point out that Melaleuca is not "marketing a marketing plan." His emphasis is on product—always on product. He constantly reminds his Marketing Executives that, without quality products, Melaleuca is nothing—"We have no excuse to be here."[1]

Given his emphasis on quality in products, it becomes apparent just how much he was impressed by the potential of melaleuca oil when it was first introduced to him by the Ball brothers. For a man to latch onto a single product with which to

9

drive an entire marketing plan, he has to be very, very impressed by its capabilities. And rightly so. Melaleuca oil is a unique substance with very unique properties.

The Re-Discovery of Melaleuca Oil, "Nature's Wonder"

The story of melaleuca oil goes back not tens of years nor hundreds, but millions of years, when the Melaleuca alternifolia tree first found a footing in the forbidding landscape of ancient Australia. In order to survive, the tree had to fight off many insects and diseases. It is said, "That which does not kill us makes us strong," and such is the case with the Melaleuca alternifolia tree. Over millions of years, it evolved a natural defense against these attackers by storing an oil in its leaves. This oil is a powerful substance.

The Aborigines, in particular the *Bundjalung*, knew of the tree's disinfecting and healing properties. They used it for a multitude of ailments, from insect bites to septic wounds. Captain James Cook, the first European to explore Australia, observed the Aborigines brewing a tea from its leaves. He gave the tree its common name—*Tea Tree*. At the beginning of this century, researchers confirmed the oil's antiseptic and therapeutic properties. In World War II, it became an important item in the first-aid kits of Australian soldiers.

The Aborigines, in particular the Bundjalung, knew of the tree's disinfecting and healing properties.

Over the years, the properties of the oil have been tested and proven by numerous researchers. The question is not whether it works, but what are its possible uses? So far, they seem numerous. Even the Australians have not fully investigated its capabilities, saying, "The final uses of melaleuca oil lie in the hands of the research biochemists."[2] These biochemists are actively seeking out new applications for the oil.

In 1992, Dr. Alvin Shemesh, a Harvard-trained physician practicing in California, reported his findings of using the oil on patients with a wide range of complaints, including thrush, throat infections, rashes, eczema, canker sores, herpes simplex and even fungus under the nails of women wearing false nails. The Australians themselves call it a "first-aid kit in a bottle," so wide are its uses.

It was an American who recognized melaleuca oil's potential and brought it to the U.S. in 1982.

With the rise of synthetic antibiotics after World War II, melaleuca oil was gradually forgotten by the rest of the world, and the Australian government paid little attention to it.

In recent years, scientists have begun to realize the limitations and side effects of man-made pharmaceuticals. More and more, educated consumers are demanding naturally-derived medicines and nutritional supplements. Yet until the 1980s, melaleuca oil was still relatively unknown except in Australia. The Australians, surprisingly, did not seem to capitalize on the incredible resource in their own backyard. It was an American who recognized melaleuca oil's potential and brought it to the U.S. in 1982.

The Balls and Oil of Melaleuca, Inc.

At Melaleuca, Inc., when credit is due, credit is given. Frank VanderSloot is very quick to acknowledge the debt owed to the Ball brothers, Roger and Allen, in the founding of Melaleuca, Inc. He has openly thanked them both for their tremendous insight in recognizing melaleuca oil's potential in the American marketplace, and for their courage in investing so much of their own money.

The Ball brothers are blessed with very different personal

11

qualities. Roger is of the entrepreneurial spirit, with a keen eye for new ventures. Allen is a "facts-and-figures" man, ever demanding the "bottom line." A cautious man, not swayed by his emotions, Allen tends to keep his feet planted firmly on the ground. He is a stickler for detail and demands quality in his business practice. It is a marriage of bright entrepreneurial spirit with down-to-earth solidarity. This combination made the brothers prime candidates to realize the market potential of melaleuca oil.

Roger stumbled across it on a visit to Australia in 1982, and when he broke the news on his return, even his ever-cautious brother could see its potential.

Roger is of the entrepreneurial spirit, with a keen eye for new ventures. Allen is a "facts-and-figures" man, ever demanding the "bottom line."

A period of testing was initiated in their hometown of Idaho Falls at a small laboratory, B&V Technology. They were overjoyed at the results. It seemed that melaleuca oil was not only a major antiseptic, but it possessed numerous therapeutic properties and very few, if any, side effects.

The brothers knew they were on to something. They located an Australian ranch owner in a position to give them an incredible edge in the market. This gentleman claimed an 80% control of all the Melaleuca alternifolia trees in the world.

It was a fortuitous turn of events. A wonderful natural product plus a worldwide monopoly of the supply—it was an opportunity too good to miss. The Ball brothers did not hesitate. They invested in a 50% share of the Australian ranch and set about constructing a marketing plan to sell the product throughout America.

They chose a marketing structure modeled after that of a multi-level corporation. Initially, it did very well. They talked to families and companies all over America and were able to enroll many new distributors who were excited by the prospect of a global monopoly. The business took off and in the first five months, sales were up to $90,000 a month.

Unfortunately, both brothers became pressed for time, owing to the weight of their other business commitments. There was a serious need for an experienced businessman who could take over the reins and steer the company into further success.

Immediately Frank VanderSloot's name was raised.

Frank was a friend, and Roger, ever the entrepreneur, had often contacted Frank with business proposals. Roger was renowned for having his hand in a number of start-up businesses at any one time. Frank VanderSloot had never been attracted to any of Roger's previous proposals, even though they were old friends.

Frank had come a long way since his humble Idaho origins. He was now no less than the Regional Vice President for the *Fortune* 500 company, Cox Communications. He loved the television and cable industry, and he and his family had settled down in Vancouver, Washington. Thus, when Roger Ball proposed that he join the new company, Frank showed little interest at first. His own job supplied all his needs, and by that time, he and his family were well-settled in Washington. There was no real motivation for Frank to give up his successful position for this unknown quantity no matter how well it seemed to be doing.

There was a serious need for an experienced businessman who could take over the reins and steer the company into further success.

Roger persisted in his efforts to bring Frank onto the team. It is a measure of his enthusiasm that, eventually, he succeeded.

Frank agreed to meet up with the the Balls in Phoenix, Arizona. At the meeting, Frank was introduced to the Australian ranch owner and the three officially extended an offer for him to join the company. Frank, though impressed by their enthusiasm, was not too easily wooed into taking up a new venture on hearsay—he was too seasoned a businessman. He declined to comment until he had fully investigated the product himself.

As he became aware of the unique qualities of this ancient, natural product, his enthusiasm grew by leaps and bounds.

His own investigations did the trick. As he became aware of the unique qualities of this ancient, natural product, his enthusiasm grew by leaps and bounds. Finally, he weighed the prospects, and decided to accept the offer.

The Ball brothers were overjoyed. Having someone of Frank's experience in charge of the project not only gave them more time to take care of their other business interests, but they had absolute confidence in Frank's capabilities. Thus they gave him a totally free hand. Frank was left to take care of the business, then known as "Oil of Melaleuca, Inc."

Frank obviously had great plans for the company. He had studied the product, he knew the American market and he was certain he was onto a winner, so he devoted himself to this new venture with a burning zeal.

Major Problems, Unforeseen Difficulties

Over the next few months it became apparent that the structure of the new company was, to say the least, far from ideal. It was apparent that the Ball brothers, busy men pressed for time, had adopted a business plan which they may have thought twice about had they realized its full implications.

Though the company's revenue had reached a promising

$90,000 per month in the first five months, this was mainly based on a business practice which VanderSloot began to question—the fact that a distributor was encouraged to purchase and sell large inventories of expensive Starter Kits. Soon the young company was plagued by problems that neither Frank nor the Ball brothers could have foreseen. The rising profits peaked, then began falling rapidly.

The distributors were becoming very annoyed. Some of them had large amounts invested in hundreds of Starter Kits which they couldn't sell. The "front-end loading" on which this system was based had been copied from the business practice of another company. The Ball brothers had not investigated its legal validity because the business plan was already in use. As it turned out, it was actually illegal in all fifty states!

He had burned his bridges behind him and now the initial success of Oil of Melaleuca, Inc. was rapidly turning into a business disaster.

It could have been a distressing experience for Frank. He had burned his bridges behind him and now the initial success of Oil of Melaleuca, Inc. was rapidly turning into a business disaster. But he was made of sterner stuff than that and he set out to remedy these problems as best he could.

Another problem suddenly reared its head. The products themselves began to manifest side-effects which were highly undesirable. Some of them had a smell which was offensive, and some were slightly caustic and stinging. As a result, of the eight new products launched under Oil of Melaleuca, four had to be withdrawn from the market.

Frank realized that the Ball brothers had not intentionally launched substandard products. He trusted them. The fact was, the products had been formulated by people who were inexperienced with melaleuca oil, and in formulating skin care and cosmetic products.

Another problem came up. Before Frank arrived, some promotional materials had been produced and distributed which advertised melaleuca oil as a cure for a wide variety of medical conditions. Although some of these claims had been validated by research and documented in other countries, they could not be made in the U.S. because they had not been validated by the FDA themselves. Frank soon learned it was illegal to make any medical claims about his product until official approval was given by the FDA. He was determined to conduct business in a completely legal and ethical manner. So he immediately took steps to take all illegal literature out of circulation.

Frank and the Ball brothers hastily severed ties with the Australian and the agonizing decision was made to close the company.

Frank had unwittingly taken over the helm of a vessel that was sailing into treacherous waters. Then came the final blow, and the good ship Oil of Melaleuca, Inc. hit the rocks and sank. The claims of an 80% world monopoly on the oil turned out to be completely false. Their Australian partner had only about 5% of the world's Melaleuca alternifolia trees on his own property!

It was nothing short of a major disaster. Frank and the Ball brothers hastily severed ties with the Australian and the agonizing decision was made to close the company. The promise of a soaring meteorite of marketing success had fizzled out into a damp pile of ashes. In its wake it left the Ball brothers with considerable financial losses and Frank without a job.

Frank's reaction to this plight is a prime example for any Marketing Executive of how to deal with failure. Frank did not curse, tear his hair out, or proceed to blame everyone and everybody in sight—as is often the case in business. He did exactly the opposite. He used these trying experiences as lessons from which he could learn a more viable approach. He said, "Those were the most valuable five months of my business career. In those five months, I learned more about people and their needs and feelings and hopes and dreams than I did in my entire business career or four years at college."[3]

Frank realized that the Ball brothers had been sincere but misled. He thought about starting a new company of his own, he was so convinced he could turn this lemon into lemonade. He had always wanted to form a company based on his own principles, and he had saved his money over the years for just such an opportunity. But the Ball brothers were not ready to throw in the towel either. They still believed the oil was a great product and would sell. But they knew they needed VanderSloot, with the special knowledge he had acquired and his management exper-

"In those five months, I learned more about people and their needs and feelings and hopes and dreams than I did in my entire business career or four years at college."

tise, if the business was to succeed. The Balls asked VanderSloot to join them in starting a brand new company.

VanderSloot agreed to form a partnership. However, he wanted to be sure that he would be able to run the company independently, his decisions fully backed by the Balls. Roger and Allen had faith in VanderSloot's personal integrity and his management skills, so they agreed to this provision. VanderSloot would be the president and CEO of the new company, which would be called Melaleuca, Inc. He invested the same amount into the business as originally invested by the Balls, and became an equal partner in the new company. This date was to become a historic landmark—September 1, 1985.

Laying the Foundation for Future Success

Using the mistakes of that first ill-fated company as examples of what *not* to do, Frank VanderSloot began to formulate a number of founding principles to ensure that Melaleuca, Inc. would never suffer the same fate.

Oil of Melaleuca, Inc. had been founded on shifting sand. The lack of a strong foundation allowed illegality, and indifference to the needs of distributors and customers, to destroy the company. Frank analyzed the root causes of the failure and, for each cause, established a principle that would avoid these pitfalls. He was convinced that a company could do well by doing right.

Frank's position at Cox had already been filled, but this was not what led him forward. In many ways, the demise of Oil of Melaleuca, Inc. was a blessing in disguise—though it must have taken some personal grit for Frank to see it like that at the time.

Frank was still absolutely convinced that melaleuca oil was a great product. Oil of Melaleuca, Inc. had folded just eight short months after its start-up. During this period, Frank had learned a great deal about the skin-care industry. He had already been working on some novel ideas for a marketing plan and now, here was an opportunity that he'd always wanted; the silver lining in the murky cloud of Oil of Melaleuca's failure was that he could start his own business, his own way.

His first action as Melaleuca's president was to establish a mission statement.

His first action as Melaleuca's president was to establish a mission statement. The anger and bitterness suffered by the Oil of Melaleuca, Inc. distributors who had lost so much had made a deep impression on Frank. Akin to modern doctors who take the ancient Hippocratic Oath—"first do no harm"—Frank, too,

18

was determined that he would do no harm. He swore that Melaleuca would never hurt anybody, neither its Marketing Executives nor its customers.

He took this goal even further. It was not enough that Melaleuca would not hurt anybody. Frank wanted a business that would actively enhance the quality of life of all those involved. This is a very key issue for Frank VanderSloot. It is not a business approach but a deep-felt personal statement. He said, "Simply stated, it means a lot to me. It means everything to me. That what we're doing is enhancing people's lives. That no one gets hurt from what we do."[4]

"Simply stated, it means a lot to me. It means everything to me. That what we're doing is enhancing people's lives. That no one gets hurt from what we do."

The mission statement is something that will crop up again and again throughout the Melaleuca story, simply because, in many ways, it *is* the Melaleuca story. Time and time again it will be seen that whenever focus is needed within Melaleuca, it is regained by a return to the bedrock mission.

It is not an abstract slogan or a motivational rally cry. It is something so essential to the foundations of the Melaleuca experience that Frank was to say, "Contrary to other mission statements that are often framed in a beautiful oak frame and hung in a corporate hallway somewhere to be forgotten, everyone knows what our mission is. Every employee knows it. Every Marketing Executive knows it. It has been very effective in guiding our activities and our focus, and it has been very rewarding as we accomplish its message: 'To enhance the lives of those we touch by helping people reach their goals.'"[5]

In the brief period before Oil of Melaleuca, Inc. folded, Frank had not only learned about the skin-care industry, he had learned a lot about FDA regulations and laws. He had already been formulating a marketing plan. Now, armed with a little experience, a little knowledge and major ideas for a marketing plan, Frank took the bit between his teeth. He was determined that Melaleuca, Inc. would never violate state or federal laws.

He embarked on a quest to seek out information and quality products. He talked to FDA attorneys, corporate attorneys and multi-level attorneys alike. Before adding anything to his marketing plan, he would consult marketing gurus, business wizards and direct sales experts, leaving no stone unturned in his search for information that would enable him to create the ultimate marketing plan.

In amassing the advice from these experts, Frank did not always follow their recommendations. He took what he thought best and incorporated it into his own vision. If it did not fit, he simply shrugged it off. For instance, the consultants advised him to adopt a system which encouraged distributors to invest initially in large inventories sold only in case lots. They also recommended that bonuses should be awarded on the basis of a high minimum monthly purchase of products.

Frank had worked on his plan for a long time, often late into the night, perfecting its details.

This was a little too much like the scheme that had caused the downfall of the first company. Instead, Frank took an approach which, he felt, would not hurt anybody. It was a risk-free plan with a low monthly production requirement well within the scope of any household.

Frank had worked on his plan for a long time, often late into the night, perfecting its details. He brought a lifetime of business experience to construct the plan and hours of purposeful study to refine it. When it was finished, it was both innovative and visionary. Not only did it support Melaleuca's stated mission, but at the practical level, all bases were covered—financial, humane, ethical. It was a statement honed by experience and etched in granite to withstand the assaults of a tumultuous marketplace.

Helping Others to Help Themselves

At the heart of Frank's plan was an idea so basically American that it seems visionary, only because so many "traditional" businesses have lost sight of it. Namely, that the "free enterprise" system does not have to be exploitative. With careful planning, there is enough for everyone who is willing to work. Frank's form of free enterprise provided a system where families, singles and single parents, for a part-time investment of their time, not money, could meet their goals. Whatever their needs—retirement security, college fees, mortgage payoff—this supplemental income could be attained through working a Melaleuca business.

The plan structure actually rewards those who help others. It is the old way in which America was built— people helping people.

The plan structure actually rewards those who help others. It is the old way in which America was built—people helping people. Yet, there are no free rides. The idea is not to give away opportunity but to empower people to make their own.

Frank's reasoning was this: Give a man a fish, it will feed him for a day; teach him how to fish and he can feed himself for a lifetime. Stated in another way, the goal of Melaleuca—"to enhance the lives of those we touch by helping people reach their goals"—is the same as "we are teaching people how to fish."

In later years as Melaleuca took off, Frank was to make a remarkable statement about this empowerment. He told his Marketing Executives that making money had to be secondary. This didn't mean they would not make money—it was just a change of focus. Their main aim was to help other people attain their goals. Yes, money would be made. But, by keeping the focus on mutual cooperation, it eliminated any trend toward greed or self-interest. These were the factors that had sabotaged other direct sales-type businesses.

His plan would not reward those who were interested in making a quick buck by selling large inventories to new recruits. Instead, it would pay bonuses on regular monthly purchases. The participants would enroll customers who would buy only the products they needed each month. It would take time to build a business this way.

In his search, Frank met a man who had developed a superior line of natural household cleaners.

There would be no promise of quick riches, but there would be the potential for steady income over many years.

Exceptional Products at Reasonable Prices

Wary of illicit claims for products and their destructive effect on the first company, Frank was determined that not only should each product meet all the requisite standards for every regulatory agency, but that the products would be the very best on the market.

To do so, he set out to build up a network of pharmacists, chemists, nutritionists—anybody who could provide a quality product or ways to improve a product. Frank sought quality goods, from quality people, for quality people.

In his search, Frank met a man who had developed a very superior line of natural household cleaners. This man, a chemist, did not have a distribution system. A most happy marriage of mutual interests took place. Knowing the solvency properties of melaleuca oil, Frank initiated further research. As a result, melaleuca oil was added to these fine household cleaners, improving them yet again—and a new product line was born.

In his search for quality, Frank even went to Australia. There, he spent time visiting plantations, making friends and contacts, and was able to establish a steady supply of melaleuca oil from natural stands of trees which had never been treated with herbicides or pesticides.

Melaleuca oil was, of course, the cornerstone of Melaleuca's products in the early days. As Frank expanded the product line, he began seeking out other natural products free of toxic agents, with minimal impact on the environment. Working with the best pharmacists and chemists in the business, he began to perfect a new line of natural products. And so Melaleuca expanded into nutrition, personal hygiene and home hygiene—a multitude of products, naturally-based, of exceeding high quality.

Through his experiences in the data processing industry, Frank was able to incorporate a strategy into the marketing plan where the brunt of the paperwork and record-keeping would be removed from the Marketing Executives. To do this, he needed high-powered computer systems, programmed to handle hundreds of complex tasks. In order to make this happen, he needed the services of a top programmer, but he could not afford to hire one full-time. Frank had to improvise—and he did. Frank contacted one of the top programmers in the area, Dennis Otteson. A compromise was agreed upon, and Dennis worked part-time, evenings after his day job, until the program was set up in the computer and ready to go.

Through his experiences in the data processing industry, Frank was able to incorporate a strategy into the marketing plan where the brunt of the paperwork and record-keeping would be removed from the Marketing Executives.

Later, Frank achieved a ground-breaking benchmark: the

final accreditization of melaleuca oil by the FDA as a natural antiseptic and fungicide. By working closely with FDA attorneys, Frank had at last obtained its validation. Signed, sealed and fully bona fide, melaleuca oil had finally arrived in America.

Humble Beginnings— Getting the New Company Off the Ground

Frank had accomplished a great deal since the demise of Oil of Melaleuca, Inc. He had a mission statement, he had a marketing plan, and by force of diligent research, he had twenty high-quality products.

The wear and tear to get to this point would have exhausted a lesser man than Frank. But the way ahead seemed even more daunting.

Melaleuca was largely unknown, and Frank had no support team or adequate promotional material. Almost single-handed, he set about building up his business. He had already made sure the foundations were rock solid. But he needed a few more Marketing Executives to start putting up the walls. Maybe some day he'd even get a roof!

Given these circumstances, Frank's faith in his products, his plan and his ideals had to have been enormous.

Novice Marketing Executives, shaken by failure or rejection, should bear in mind that today's Melaleuca system is an extensive support network of like-minded individuals with a thirteen year track record of satisfaction and success. There was no such structure for Frank VanderSloot. In the early days, Melaleuca only had seven employees, based in Idaho Falls. Meetings were conducted by Frank VanderSloot, informational material was written by Frank VanderSloot, and it was Frank VanderSloot who monitored customer sales and manufacturing distribution. In the evening, he would go home and mobilize his family. They would all join in, stapling material, addressing envelopes and sending out the magazine to every Marketing Executive. Initially, mailing magazines was easy because there was only one Marketing Executive—Frank VanderSloot.

Secret Meetings

Given these circumstances, Frank's faith in his products, his plan and his ideals had to have been enormous. Anybody who has waited for the arrival of an audience prior to a presentation must recall that nervous, butterfly feeling that perhaps nobody would come. Well, that's exactly what happened to Frank in this painful, pioneer period—not once, but repeatedly. But he took it in his stride. He whimsically refers to his solo efforts in those early days as "secret meetings."

Unfazed, Frank plowed on, drawing strength from the qualities inherited from his father—patience, perseverance and perspiration.

He'd arrive in a strange town, book into a motel, arrange his products and his banners meticulously, then wait ... and wait. And often, no one would come. What did Frank do? Pack up, depressed? No. He would give his presentation to an empty room. "It's good practice," he would say years later, laughing at the idea.[6]

As Frank worked to expand Melaleuca, there were many such secret meetings. Unfazed, Frank plowed on, drawing strength from the qualities inherited from his father—patience, perseverance and perspiration.

Building New Fires, Fanning the Flames

In his initial attempts to enroll new Marketing Executives, Frank naturally targeted the old Oil of Melaleuca distributors. Many of the old distributors decided they didn't want to join the new company if there was no monopoly on melaleuca oil and no quick money to be made on inventory loading—an odd response considering their recent experience. Nevertheless, fired by Frank's vision and the quality of the new products, a few did make the transition to Melaleuca, Inc. Frank's integrity and reputation also played a major role in the enrollment of these faithful few.

And faith was an essential commodity. Joe and Sandy Wise, pioneer Melaleuca Marketing Executives, recall these days with nostalgia and a hint of awe that so much has been accomplished since then. "In the old days, we'd have meetings at the Idaho Falls Science Center," Joe remembers.

"Frank said there would be people in this company making thousands of dollars ... we sometimes found that a little hard to believe." "Sometimes thirty people would show up in the middle of a blizzard. Frank said there would be people in this company making thousands of dollars ... we sometimes found that a little hard to believe. But here we are ... it has all come true. For a few years, Melaleuca was just a bud; but now it's [flowered] into something spectacular."[7]

Similar sentiments were expressed by Rob and Sherri Dias. They recall hosting a meeting in Ogden, Utah, which turned out to be "secret"—that is, zero attendance. Frank had come down to Ogden, and Sherri and Rob chatted with him prior to the (non)arrival of the audience.

Obviously this was a nervous time for novices Rob and Sherri, but even in those circumstances, they were both impressed by Frank's optimism despite the no-show. "He made some really prophetic statements as we talked," says Sherri, "He said that we would grow by thousands of people a month one day. Frank told Rob: 'One day, Rob, when you are eighty years old and you have your cane and you're hobbling to the mailbox,

I guarantee there will be a Melaleuca check there."[8]

Nowadays, Melaleuca is flourishing, but these pioneer Marketing Executives are remembered fondly by Frank. He openly applauds their efforts, so crucial to the building of the company at a time when faith was all they had. Without marketing literature, without the bonuses and incentives of present-day Melaleuca, Marketing Executives such as Bonnie and Larry Alexander operated on little more than a wing and a prayer.

Frank is not a man to forget this kind of loyalty. During one of his public addresses, he thanked these Marketing Executives personally. "They had hope and faith and confidence and they stood up and led, and the sales came in. That start is basically what we've built this business on."[9]

Of those Marketing Executives who had such an enormous impact on the expansion of Melaleuca, not all came into the company with faith and positivity. In fact, two of the most influential couples initially came to Melaleuca with an attitude of hostility and suspicion.

Wayne Winters arrived at Idaho Falls unannounced, declaring, "I want to see Frank VanderSloot and I want to see him now!"

Wayne Winters arrived at Idaho Falls unannounced, declaring, "I want to see Frank VanderSloot and I want to see him now!" Wayne was determined to dissuade his wife Gwen from staying with Melaleuca, convinced it was a waste of time, not to mention money.[10]

Ron and Camille Frasure were responsible for enrolling the Winters in May of 1987. The Frasures had enrolled the previous month after a disappointing stint with Amway. It's interesting that Ron actually set out to prove to one of his Amway prospects that Melaleuca was not a legitimate opportunity. His prospect had enrolled in Melaleuca, much to his dismay, and he was determined that he would find a problem with the program, and talk her out of it. "All these things that come through town, these multi-level businesses, they're all pretty much scams," Ron explains. "And if you just simply look at them with an objective point of view, you're going to find a red flag sticking up. ... I wanted to find out some details to save these people who were obviously making a mistake."

What happened next was not what Ron had expected. He studied the business carefully in order to discredit it, and the opposite happened. "I was impressed. After I saw it, I got excited."[11]

The conversion of the Frasures and the Winters from doubters to doers had an enormous effect on Melaleuca's growth, visibly evident in the growth chart of the company from that period. Every one of those early pioneers has been thanked by Frank. Though he always credits his Marketing Executives with the growth of Melaleuca, he never mentions that it was his confidence and positivity that enabled them to get so far. His hands-on involvement and his constant reassurance began to fan the flames, and his total enthusiasm was to set many a reluctant Marketing Executive on fire.

"I was impressed. After I saw it, I got excited."

Rob Dias illustrates Frank's commitment to the Melaleuca community by recalling the time when there was a problem with the processing of the Marketing Executives' monthly checks. The possibility of a delay in sending the checks out bothered Frank tremendously. He was, and still is, proud of the fact that the company has never been late with a commission check in its history. Of course, Marketing Executives liked to get their checks on time, and due to processing problems, it was obvious that this was not going to happen. Frank took care of it personally. Every check for every Marketing Executive arrived right on time—because he mailed each one of them by overnight express.

In establishing Melaleuca as a business to last a lifetime, Frank tapped into a secret long known to the statesmen and leaders of today and of yesteryear as well. That is, when people are working toward a common goal with shared values in an organization which they respect, and are respected, everything is possible. Each person will give 100%, 200% or even 300%, not because they have to, but because they want to.

Frank's enthusiasm provided the initial spark; his Marketing Executives fanned the flames and now Melaleuca is a bright, beaming light in the twilight of the 90's.

Frank was told he would fail. People said his aims were impossible. Some of his Marketing Executives

Some of his Marketing Executives believed it was not possible to attain the status of Executive Director.

believed it was not possible to attain the status of Executive Director, which requires about 1,000 preferred customers. Inspired by Frank and their faith in the products, Rob and Sherri Dias did it, then Ron and Camille Frasure. The flames, fueled by positivity, spread to Wayne and Gwen Winters—and even further. Now there are hundreds of people who have reached the level of Executive Director in Melaleuca.

By acting as a role model, by having the faith to overcome the tremendous obstacles encountered initially, by building his organization on sound principles such that nothing could shake it, Frank has taken Melaleuca from its humble revenue of $230,000 in 1985 to over $300 million in just eleven years.

The success of Melaleuca has not gone unnoticed in the business world. Each year the Blue Chip Enterprise Award is presented to two hundred small businesses chosen from tens of thousands as part of The Blue Chip Enterprise Initiative Program. The award was given to Melaleuca in 1991 because of the management's "ability to meet tremendous challenges and overcome adversity."[12]

Every year, *Inc.* magazine produces an index of the five hundred fastest-growing, privately-held companies in America. *Inc.* says of these companies, "Behind the typical *Inc.* 500 company is a great story about personal triumph, economic growth and job creation, and in front of them lies the future of the new economy."[13]

Although it was a generalized statement, it could have been written specifically about Melaleuca. Melaleuca is one of the few companies to appear on *Inc.* 500's index five years in a row. In addition, Melaleuca is the first company to maintain an "A" rating for profit each of those five years. In the year when the aforementioned quote appeared, Melaleuca was rated as #4 in the nation in absolute dollar growth, and #5 in job creation.

The scope of Frank VanderSloot's achievements is truly awe-inspiring. Yet, typically modest, he points to his Marketing Executives as being the driving force behind Melaleuca's success. In particular, he applauds those early pioneers who stuck with Melaleuca when the going was tough.

The very fact of Frank's humility in view of his accomplishments singles him out as an exceptional human being. But he does not want to be considered remarkable; his contention is that very ordinary people are capable of extraordinary feats. Despite his modesty, his personal achievements indicate that Frank has within his resources a tremendous font of spiritual power. He claims that such power is available to everybody and that one person can make a tremendous difference in the lives of many others. He calls it the "Power of One."

CHAPTER 2

The Power of One

"I am only one. But still I am one.
I cannot do everything but still I can do something;
And because I cannot do everything
I will not refuse to do the something I can do."

—Edward Evert

 The power of one person.

Can one person make a difference? Ask among your friends and no doubt they will think a little, and then the names will come: Einstein, Ghandi, Mother Teresa, Martin Luther King. Of course, the achievements of these famous people were enormous. But in looking at the principles with which Frank VanderSloot formed the foundations of Melaleuca, Inc., when he talks about the "power of one," he means it in a slightly different way. No doubt Mr. VanderSloot would be the first to applaud the achievements of these famous humanitarians. But when Frank VanderSloot talks about the "power of one," he isn't just thinking about important, powerful people; he is talking about you or me—all of us.

Throughout his writing and public addresses, there is a constant theme. Sometimes it is obvious, sometimes it lies

31

buried in the core of his address, not really seen but pulsing in every fiber of the speech. It is a theme that springs from his own humble origins—that ordinary people have great power and you don't have to be famous or incredibly gifted to make this world a better place. "We don't have to do great, newsworthy things to have a great influence on this world. We only need to live a life others can follow. It is impossible to measure the impact that one life can have on thousands of others."[1]

There is a compelling strength behind these assertions of Frank VanderSloot—and it is the resonance of conviction. He is not preaching; that is not his way. Rather, he is sharing beliefs that were fundamental to his own personal formation. Despite his modest claims to the contrary, Frank is an extraordinary person and his tremendous faith in the power of ordinary people adds to this. It's an odd paradox, but all his attempts to distance himself from the lofty position of "leader" have the opposite effect. "I don't see myself as any guru—I'm not. I accept the responsibility of making hard decisions, ... I accept the responsibility that sometimes I need to say no ... I will be worthy of your trust ... I promise you that I will put my whole heart and soul into this business, and keeping it safe and prosperous for all of you and all of our families," he says.[2]

"We don't have to do great, newsworthy things to have a great influence on this world. We only need to live a life others can follow."

Therein lies the power of Melaleuca, the power of Frank VanderSloot, and the power of each one of the Melaleuca Marketing Executives—the knowledge that the average person can have an enormous effect on the lives of others. And no illustration could serve better than the example of Frank VanderSloot's own development.

In order to realize how Frank's lessons in life came to form the mighty pillars of the Melaleuca principles, we need to turn to a story within our story. It began many years ago in a small farmhouse near to the town of Cocolalla, Idaho ...

Embracing a Father's Influence

It's late afternoon on a country road. The shadows lengthen as dusk falls. A school bus draws up and deposits a boy on the side of the road. As it roars away, he waves goodbye and begins to trudge along the road. Ahead of him are the cheery lights of a small farmhouse. His pace quickens.

He is about ten, with an open, pleasant face and an upright stance. His clothes, purchased at Salvation Army and Goodwill thrift stores, are worn but neat, evidence of many washings. He walks with even strides, obviously a little tired.

The boy's name is Frank. His mind is busy. His mind is always busy—that's his character. In the isolation of the farm, he has little time or opportunity to share his inner thoughts. Even now, he is thinking about the chores he has to do. It's been an hour-long bus journey home from school, but still there's a fence to be fixed, Mom will want help with the potatoes, and there's always cows to be milked and other animals to tend to. He sighs. There's not too much time for anything else apart from work and sleep. He's glad it's Friday. Perhaps he'll have some time to himself over the weekend. He sees the old 1957 Rambler station wagon parked round the side of the house. Dad's back home! He's been away for a week. Frank's face splits into a broad smile and he leaps onto the porch as he runs to greet his father.

Later ...

Frank sits down to eat with his two sisters and older brother. Father sits at the head of the table, obviously tired after a long week. The food, though simple, is nutritious. Frank is endowed

33

with the healthy appetite of a growing boy. Hunger makes a good sauce. They begin to eat; there's little conversation, though the two younger girls venture a whisper here and there. Frank's older brother is largely silent. Eating is serious business. Mr. VanderSloot is a gnarled, wiry man with the hands of a laborer and the tough, lean body of a man who has worked all his life. He, too, eats in silent enjoyment. Finally, with a sigh of appreciation, Mr. VanderSloot pushes back his plate and Mrs. VanderSloot ventures into conversation: Had he heard about the house that had burned down in Sandpoint? The topic is immediately of interest to all at the table. This is rural Idaho and Sandpoint is the nearest town. A fire is a top news item.

"Wow!" he exclaims, "I would love to see a house burn down!"

Frank, who as usual is fidgeting, his mind racing over a score of topics, cannot contain himself. He has always been fascinated by fire. "Wow!" he exclaims, "I would love to see a house burn down!"

The excitement in his tone makes Mr. VanderSloot turn to stare thoughtfully at Frank. He takes in the flushed face, the brightness in the boy's eyes, and a dark shadow comes over his own face as he remembers Frank's habit of playing with matches. He says nothing. Nor does he speak much for the rest of the evening. Bedtime comes very rapidly. Wake-up time is 5:30 a.m. the next day.

Next morning ...

Frank walks across the yard, shivering slightly. The sun is not yet up. Though the pink fingers of dawn are edging up over the distant horizon, there is a chill in the air. Frank has finished his chores. He pours the last bucket into the large milk churn and wipes the sticky remains of milk from his palms. He stops as his father beckons him and together they walk around to a little lot behind the chicken coop. Mr. VanderSloot is carrying a saw, hammer and some nails. Frank glances down at them, puzzled.

His father, a quiet, even man, catches the glance. "We're going to build a house," he says.

Frank is thrilled. They set about the task diligently. They work at it all day. By the time they finish, the sun is beginning to disappear over the horizon. Measuring about five by three feet, the house stands three feet tall with a chimney, windows and a real porch. It even has a tiny picket fence. To a ten-year-old country boy, it is quite a work of art.

As they stand admiring their masterpiece, his father says, "OK son, burn it down." Frank looks at him, perplexed. Is he joking? "Let's burn it down, son," repeats the father. He is not joking. Frank, his mind racing, runs to fetch the matches thinking about his own words of the night before.

As they stand admiring their masterpiece, his father says, "OK son, burn it down."

He returns, walking slowly, his mind in a turmoil. It is a fine house ... they had made it together, he and his Dad. Now ... burn it down? It seems such a waste.

"OK, burn it down," says his father.

Frank hesitates, torn by emotion. His father motions toward the house with his hand. Frank lets out a sigh and, kneeling down, begins to heap some twigs and leaves near the fireplace inside their beautiful house. With mixed feelings, he sets it on fire.

Frank and his father stand silently and watch their work slowly go up in flames until it is rendered to ashes. It is a silent, wordless lesson, more compelling, more memorable than a statement.

As they walk away from the pile of hot ashes—all that is left of their creativity—Mr. VanderSloot puts his arm around the boy. "Well, son, you've seen a house burn down now. Is that kind of what you wanted? Do you feel that you need to see any more homes burn down?"

"No Dad," says Frank.

"Great son," says Mr. VanderSloot.

The lesson, imposed with humility, kindness and understanding, had left its mark—permanently.[3]

And that was the way of his father, Peter Francis VanderSloot. With only a third-grade education, he worked up to sixty hours a week on the railways, sometimes away a week at a time. His life was spent solely in feeding his kids and supporting his home. And yet, Mr. VanderSloot was possessed of that quiet wisdom about things that matter. Such is the way of all those who tend horses, love animals, till the soil and work hard for a living.

"If I had not had the influence of my father in my life, ... it's doubtful that Melaleuca would exist as it does today."

To this day, Frank VanderSloot holds up his father as an example of a great person, a naturally wise man. So much so, that in one public address, he said "If I had not had the influence of my father in my life, ... it's doubtful that Melaleuca would exist as it does today."[4]

In his President's Message given in September 1996, Frank explored the theme "the power of one." He said, "My father's life is a great reminder of the power of that principle. A single person *can* make a difference—a tremendous difference."[5]

VanderSloot's father died in 1982, before Melaleuca was founded, so he never saw how far his son had taken these principles. Mr. VanderSloot had done a fine job. Though he said little, it's obvious he never missed much. In his quiet way, he had planted the seeds of his own wisdom in Frank. A thorough man, he'd done a thorough job. But of course, it would take time for these seeds to grow.

"I Just Wanted to Be the Garbage Man"

Mr. VanderSloot's contribution to Frank's development cannot be underestimated. The qualities he instilled in Frank were so deep that they became the mainstay of the Melaleuca culture—honesty, understatement, living within your means, and above all, being free of debt.

Though these values were implanted deeply in Frank, at first, they did not flourish. Frank's story is not of a shooting star, brighter than all its peers, zooming to a crescendo of stellar success. On the contrary, when Frank first ventured into the public arena of school, he was a shy, retiring boy with no desire whatsoever to take initiative. Initially, *One day, Frank was called to his office. The principal was concerned about his response to a test.* he was a lackluster student with no leadership skills. But due to the intervention of a few key figures, the wisdom implanted by his father did flourish.

To appreciate this transformation from shy country boy to resilient leader, we have to pick up the story again when Frank was a freshman in high school.

The adolescent years are often a time of emotional turmoil and moody introspection. It is a time when teenagers are beginning to actively question themselves. It is the stage when they begin discovering who they are, sometimes with a dreamy awareness, sometimes with a sense of discomfort or pain. With it comes a growing sense of the mystery of life, of the bridge between adolescence and manhood.

Frank VanderSloot's introspective process needed a boost, however, and this was given by Mr. Stidwell, his principal. One day, Frank was called to his office. The principal was concerned about his response to a test. Mr. Stidwell, though stern and intimidating to the shy young Frank, also had a keen eye and a sense of empathy which enabled him to point Frank in the right direction without a word of admonishment or criticism. The *way* in which people helped Frank was to become very important to him in his adult life. When speaking on this topic to Melaleuca Marketing Executives, he said, "Helping does not mean pushing or coercing or convincing. Helping does not mean badgering nor does is mean doing it for them. We are in the business of teaching men and women how to fish, not giving them fish."[6]

"All of these questions have to do with leadership. You are answering that way because you don't want to be in front of anyone, do you?"

In some way, Mr. Stidwell seemed to have understood the needs of the nervous young man who came into his office. He never actually gave Frank any direct advice. He did not say Frank had to do something about his "wallflower" trait. Nevertheless, this meeting had a profound effect on Frank—and something concrete did materialize.

One section of the test Frank took was aimed at determining students' "desire to be a leader." It was a kind of *attitude* test rather than an *aptitude* test; a "what-do-you-want-to-do-when-you-grow-up kind of test," Frank later recalled. One question revolved around a fictional situation in which the student was asked how he would best go about solving a town's garbage problem. There were various levels at which he could choose to step in and solve the problem. The highest point of intervention was to take the role of Mayor. Then there were choices down through the various ranks to the lowest—the man who picks up the garbage. Frank responded to the question by choosing to be the garbage man.

Without badgering, the principal gently began to probe Frank to find out why he'd settled for the role of bottom dog. "All of these questions have to do with leadership," said Mr. Stidwell. "You are answering that way because you don't want to be in front of anyone, do you?"

"No sir," replied Frank.

The principal then asked Frank why it scared him so, but Frank had no answer—he just repeated, "I don't know. I just don't like to be in front of people, sir."[7]

The principal was a good teacher and a shrewd man. Frank was dismissed without further discussion. The principal had achieved what he wanted—he left Frank with enough so that Frank could tackle the problem himself. Mr. Stidwell had achieved something which was later to become a basic principle in Melaleuca: Mr. Stidwell had given Frank the means to help himself.

"The magic is in helping others reach their goals and not in trying to reach our own goals."

As head of Melaleuca, Frank stresses this point repeatedly: "... the magic is in helping others reach their goals and not in trying to reach our own goals."[8] And the idea has spread. Since Melaleuca was formed, thousands have joined the ranks and have gotten caught up in the idea of helping others. Frank VanderSloot, in drawing from his own experiences, has tapped something fundamental in human nature. By focusing on the success of others, Melaleuca Marketing Executives have formed a climate where prosperity and success is shared by all who are willing to work. And the wisdom which enabled Frank to incorporate this came from those early figures who helped him discover himself—the "power of one" again.

Principal Stidwell's input may seem negligible, he was so subtle. But the result was that Frank *himself* began to ponder the question—"Why don't I want to be in front of people?" Frank began to think back. He took himself on a mental journey through various incidents in his life. As he did so, he slowly began to realize what had happened. Not one but a number of incidents had contributed to his shyness. As he turned these events over in his mind, Frank was amazed to realize how much he'd been conditioned by simple events in the past. It was his own journey of self-discovery which would lead him to the true principles of leadership.

A Journey of Self Discovery

Dr. Francine Shapiro, Ph.D., is the founder of an amazing breakthrough therapy for stress and trauma named EMDR. This process is so novel that it was featured on *20/20* by Barbara Walters. The significance of this to our story is her discussion of how "blocks" are set up in individuals by different kinds of unpleasant incidents.

It was his own journey of self-discovery which would lead him to the true principles of leadership.

"*Big T*" trauma, as she calls it, is often life-threatening—kidnapping, assault, earthquake, fire. These can undermine a person's ability to cope, resulting in intense fear or depression and loss of control. This is not relevant here. But something she terms "*Small T,*" or minor trauma, *is* relevant and it is what each and every one of us has had to go through in our lives.

"Small T trauma occurs in the innocuous but upsetting experiences that daily life sends our way," she says. "It can result in some of the same feelings as Big T trauma—and have far-reaching consequences."[9]

This is not to say that Frank VanderSloot was "traumatized" in childhood. His experiences were similar to those experienced by all of us; the rude awakenings which have become known as "experience" or "the school of hard knocks." The quotation from Dr. Shapiro is just a reminder that *every one* of us had such "unpleasantnesses" in our early life. Furthermore, the effect of these apparently minor incidents is far beyond the magnitude of the experience. This can hamper us in ways which we may find hard to believe. Some people never realize how much they are being limited by the events from early life.

Frank, in exploring the reasons why he tended to opt out of the leadership role, was astounded by the apparent simplicity of the root causes. In order to fully understand what happened, we have to look closely at the conditions in which they occurred.

When Frank first started school, his social life had previously been very limited. It revolved mainly around his older brother and two younger sisters.

When Frank first started school, his social life had previously been very limited. It revolved mainly around his older brother and two younger sisters—the nearest neighborhood child was three miles away. School placed him in a kind of social contact which was very new and probably very intimidating. Every parent knows how traumatic the first day at school can be to a child, let alone one whose life had been spent in woods and dales with dogs, horses and chickens as his companions. Imagine how it must have felt for Frank to find himself in the presence of a number of strangers; older, seemingly more sophisticated boys.

Frank was obviously a strong boy and, despite his apprehension, on that very first day he joined in a baseball game. He had never played baseball with a group of children, though he knew how to whack a flying object with a stick. So he had to watch closely to pick up the rules. At first he seemed to have grasped the principles of the game. When it was his turn to bat, he hit that ball with all the determination of a young boy out to show his merit to the world. Well, it was a heck of a whack. The ball was sent sailing in a tremendous arc way out into the blue. Frank ran to first base, then second base. He turned to see where the ball was. It wasn't on its way back yet, so he turned around, ran to third base and, in blissful ignorance of the correct procedure, went back to the end of the batting line without touching home plate.

You can imagine how good he felt in that moment, having achieved such a monumental hit in front of those intimidating strangers. His joy was short lived. *They went over to Frank and forcibly dragged him over to home plate and threw him down on it.* The other boys on his team, who really wanted to win, became angry. They felt Frank had let them down. Young children can sometimes be rather cruel, and they went over to Frank and forcibly dragged him over to home plate and threw him down on it.

Nothing is greater music to a young child's ears than the applause of his peers. But nothing is more hurtful than their mockery. That's what happened. Instead of praise, his efforts were rewarded with laughter and jeers. On his very first day at school, just a young child, Frank was humiliated. He became the butt of everyone's joke for doing something they considered "stupid."

It was not a happy start to his education. And this was not the only incident that contributed to young Frank's shyness.

Mrs. Howell's Class

Frank's responsibilities in terms of time and home chores meant that he had little time to explore the social skills and bonding that are part of a young boy's life. After rising at 5:30 a.m. to milk cows, Frank had to travel an hour to school, then an hour back at night to more chores, dinner and bed. This is not a situation in which school friendships can flourish. Though everyone grew to like Frank, he had little time to develop relationships or to join in school sports where his physical skills would have given him an edge.

Added to this, Frank had an unfortunate characteristic which caused him a lot of trouble—he was endowed with an overactive mind. In modern schools, this might have been recognized as a sign of above-average ability. Unfortunately, in Frank's school days, such subtleties were not even considered. Frank found it very difficult to sit still for hours at a small desk. It is a common problem, but when it is not recognized for what it is, a sad fate is visited upon such children—they are punished so frequently that they fall below average. Their overactivity is seen as "bad behavior" and not signs of an intelligent mind bored with insufficient or inappropriate stimulus. It is a common problem in both urban and rural schools when a teacher has to deal with a large number of restless children, often of different ages and skill levels.

Frank had an unfortunate characteristic which caused him a lot of trouble — he was endowed with an overactive mind.

Frank does not blame Mrs. Howell, his teacher. In his recollections, he says she was "quite decent." He also emphasizes that he was not a bad or belligerent child. But because Frank was continually being reprimanded for his restlessness, he was beginning to feel that, as he was always in the wrong, there was something wrong with *him*. This situation tends to have a very detrimental effect on the one area in which a child needs to be nurtured—self-esteem. And Frank's self-esteem suffered badly.

Frank was not a bad child, yet the humiliation and punishment he received added to his withdrawal and lack of desire to stand out in public. And no wonder. A child who is constantly meeting a barrage of "no" or "don't" or "you shouldn't" begins to feel that he can never be right. If this is not counterbalanced by praise, it is very demoralizing. This is the power of negative reinforcement.

Though he does not refer to many parallels in his own experiences, it is obvious that somewhere down the line, Frank has had his fair share of negative reinforcement. He brought this problem to the attention of the Marketing Executives in a speech at the 1994 Melaleuca convention, where he talked of the damaging effects of negative reinforcement—and its solution, which he termed:

The Magic of Celebrating Success

In his closing remarks to the conference, Frank gave many examples of how positive support, or lack of it, can influence performance tremendously. For example, basketball games in which the motivation of the players falls off because the fans do not celebrate the players' successes. Frank points to that well-known phenomenon of the "home-court advantage," where the high-spirited support of fans and the security of the home court bolsters the home team such that they usually win. He relates this to its opposite—where low self-esteem results from being met continually with rejection and the word "no."

"We all want to know we are OK. We all want to know we did something good."

Drawing from these examples, he urges the Marketing Executives to actively applaud each other's success no matter how minor.

"We all want to know we are OK," he says. "We all want to know we did something good. There's so much negative feedback we get on a daily basis."[10]

Most eloquently, Frank begins to build a picture of how every growing child is squashed down by constant negativity. From kindergarten to adult years, the process continues—self-esteem is eroded, and guilt and self-doubt are set up by the barrage of negative feedback. Frank lists the harsh words and actions experienced by the child in his pre-school years:

"Why are you sleeping in so late? Get up."

"Oh, you spilled your milk again, dang it. Why are you so clumsy?"

"Clean that up, wash your face."

"How many times have I told you, wipe those feet!"

"Wipe your nose!"

"You embarrass me!"

"It is no better at school," says Frank. "The process continues." He is obviously talking from first-hand knowledge as he barks out the criticisms in the sharp-edged tone of an over-authoritative adult:

"Homework not done again, huh Johnny? Stay after class. Get this finished."

"This is easy. Don't you understand that?"

"Your little sister could do better than you."

"Grow up."

"You're not working fast enough."[11]

And so it goes—right into the work experience. Frank emphasizes that he is not talking about rare occasions. The problem of demoralization and negativity is common. What he wants to underscore is that only by being aware of it and actively celebrating success can it be overcome. Or the worst happens. Without self-esteem, every setback has a major impact. Drawing on his own experience, he describes two incidents, showing what a difference self-esteem can make. One occurred when he was in the 7th grade.

The Book Report

Frank stood up to deliver a book report to a class of 7th and 8th graders. His report had been well prepared because he wanted to make a good impression, but to his surprise and consternation, as he began, so did the laughter. He tried to continue but the laughter grew. Naturally, he thought it was his book report or his presentation. A most embarrassing and humiliating experience for one so nervous as Frank about speaking in public. Then one of his classmates yelled out, "Frank, your pants are unzipped!"

And this time the laughter really shook the roof and he walked back, red-faced, and sat down.

For a young man just moving into the self-conscious world of adolescence, this must have been awful. Frank reached down without looking, of course, and pulled the zipper up—and this time the laughter really shook the roof and he walked back, red-faced, and sat down.

Frank compares the agonies of this early incident with an occasion in his adult years when he went through a whole video taping and speech to a group of top Marketing Executives without realizing his fly had been undone the whole time. In fact, he didn't notice it until hours later when he was at the airport. What did he do this time? Well, he made a whimsical point about how his management team must have had a good giggle over it—and he roared with laughter. What was the difference? Frank says, "Self-esteem. Self-esteem is the stuff that greatness is made of."[12]

We all need approval, we all need self-esteem, and Frank points to an incident which occurred in his senior year at high school, which shows how one's self-esteem can be bolstered immediately, just through positive input from others.

At the high school, Frank knew all the girls on the committee in charge of putting the yearbook together. The yearbook was laid out with photos of the students. As a special tribute to each senior, the committee created a personalized caption to go under each picture. When the book came out, as any youth would do, Frank hastily searched for his own photo, wondering what fate held for him in the form of his caption. It was a pleasant surprise. It read, "Kind of nice, kind of shy, we all admit, he's our guy."[13]

It speaks well of the girls that they were able to see beyond the boundaries of his shyness. As for Frank, it did wonders for his self-esteem.

Frank felt good, but he needed a little more of a boost, and he was to receive it from a man who had a tremendous effect on his life—Peter Dalebout.

Frank did not do well his freshman year in college. He earned a lackluster 2.6 grade-point average.

Peter Dalebout was a gifted person and he took Frank under his wing after Frank's mediocre freshman year. Peter obviously saw Frank's potential and set about helping him

It read, "Kind of nice, kind of shy, we all admit, he's our guy."

in the manner that Frank has come to admire. So much so, that Frank has built it into the very fabric of Melaleuca as a principle: *Peter Dalebout helped Frank to help himself.*

"He was a self-made man," recalls Frank. "He was a believer in people, especially young people. He kind of took me under his wing. He believed in me. He made me believe in myself. I love that man because of what he gave to me."[14]

Wise in the ways of the young, Peter allowed Frank leadership roles in his organization, and other positions that enabled Frank to increase his self-esteem. Under Peter's guidance, Frank's potential began to bloom. Peter gave Frank a book,

Psycho-Cybernetics by Maxwell Maltz, a cosmetic surgeon who had tried to improve people's self-esteem through changing their appearance. Maltz found that it did not always work, and through his research into this phenomenon, gathered an amazing array of facts and insights into human motivation and the self-image. By studying this book, Frank became aware of his own limitations, and more significantly, how to overcome them.

After the experiences under Dalebout's direction, Frank continued working on his self-image and leadership skills at Ricks College. The results were gratifying. He was elected sophomore class president and president of the school Senate. He then went on to Brigham Young University, where he earned a degree in Business Administration.

"All along the way, I had men and women in my life who helped build my self-esteem."

It is obvious that under the guidance of Dalebout, Frank had blossomed—and continued to do so in his leadership skills. Having attained a measure of self-esteem from these experiences, with a growing sense of confidence, Frank went on to actualize his skills in the business world. He worked in the data processing field at Automatic Data Processing, Inc., where he was successful in turning around several regions that had been failing and taking them up to the top. But what really helped him was the fact that he was acknowledged for his accomplishments, and eventually promoted to vice-president. Later he went on to become the regional vice-president for the *Fortune* 500 company, Cox Communications, Inc.

In terms of leadership—given the original inspiration of those who'd helped him and the increased confidence that success brings—Frank was able to establish himself in the business world.

"All along the way," he says, "I had men and women in my

life who helped build my self-esteem. I believe that those people had a role in helping prepare me for the responsibilities that I now have."[15]

What had been given to him was no less than the ability to take control of his life. He reflected on this in his Thanksgiving message in 1996, which he wrote in a nostalgic frame of mind. "I am grateful for the principle of redirection—the ability that we each have of evaluating our lives and making changes within ourselves to become the best that we can be. It seems like life is a lot like driving a car: no matter where we are in life, we need to continue to make small corrections in order to keep us on the road."[16]

Frank's amazing modesty and his own "redirection" has resulted in Melaleuca, Inc., and a transformation of thousands of Melaleuca Marketing Executives' lives because of his strength and leadership.

Leadership and the "Power of One"

For a man who failed a leadership test in his youth, Frank VanderSloot has accomplished some remarkable things. He serves on the prestigious U.S. Chamber of Commerce board of directors. He also serves on the boards of the Direct Selling Association, the Direct Selling Education Foundation and the Eastern Idaho Economic Development Council. And, as if that wasn't enough, he also serves on several boards for national and international companies.

Idaho State University named Frank Idaho's Business Leader of the Year in 1998. His other awards include the Service to the Community Award, presented by the Greater Idaho Falls Area Chamber of Commerce, and the Community Enhancement Award, presented by the Blackfoot Idaho Chamber of Commerce. In the Idaho State Public Affairs Digest,

Frank is listed in the 1998 directory as one of the most influential persons in the state.

Frank's attitude to this is revealing. When he was recognized as the Idaho Business Leader of the Year, he did not want that honor solely for himself. He pointed out that Melaleuca is a team effort and that there were many people besides himself who contributed to its success—and that he was more comfortable giving out awards than receiving them. But it is no longer the young Frank VanderSloot who detested standing up in front of people who is speaking out here. Frank has discovered a new concept of leadership in the "power of one." It is the power to empower others; to enable others to do great things. His discomfort is not because he cannot stand up in public—that is no longer an issue. It is a genuine humility learned from his father, from "Peter Dalebout, who taught me to believe in myself—and so many other leaders, teachers and friends who have touched my life in so many ways."[17] When he says that the success of Melaleuca is not his alone, he means it—whatever we may think to the contrary.

Frank points to his parents who "taught me correct principles and who loved me enough to discipline me and hold me accountable for my actions."

In particular, Frank points to his parents who "taught me correct principles and who loved me enough to discipline me and hold me accountable for my actions. I am grateful for their example of hard work and of the principle of honesty and dedication to the things they believed in."[18]

Frank denies he is something special; he denies he is a guru or above average. In this very denial, Frank is revealing a quality which places him above the average leader—this is leadership par excellence. This is what the ancient sage, Lao Tzu, meant when he said "the true leader walks behind his followers."

Perhaps the most moving example of Frank's own character can be seen in the story he gave to Melaleuca Marketing Executives in May 1996 about how one person can change a life and by doing so, touch the lives of many others:

"One day at school, Jean Thompson told her students, 'Boys and girls, I love you all the same.' She knew that what she had just said was not entirely true. There was one boy whom Jean Thompson did not like. It was Teddy Stollard. Little Teddy Stollard slouched in his chair and didn't pay attention. His mouth hung open in a stupor, his eyes were always unfocused, his clothes were mussed, his hair unkempt, and he smelled. He was an unattractive boy and Jean Thompson didn't like him.

Schools have records, and Jean Thompson had Teddy's. Under the heading First grade was written: 'Teddy's a good boy. He shows promise in his work and attitude. But he has a poor home situation.' Second grade: 'Teddy is a good boy. He does what he is told. But he is too serious. His mother is terminally ill.' Third grade: 'Teddy is falling behind in his work; he needs help. His mother died this year. His father shows no interest.' Fourth grade: 'Teddy is in deep waters; he is in need of psychiatric help. He is totally withdrawn.'

Christmas came, and the boys and girls brought their presents and piled them on her desk. They were all in brightly colored paper except Teddy's. His was wrapped in brown paper and held with Scotch tape. And on it, scribbled in crayon, were the words, 'For Miss Thompson from Teddy.' She tore open the brown paper and out fell a rhinestone bracelet with most of the stones missing and a bottle of cheap perfume that was almost empty. When the other boys and girls began to giggle, she had enough sense to put some of the perfume on her wrist, put on the bracelet, hold her wrist up for the children and say, 'Doesn't it smell lovely? Isn't the bracelet pretty?' And taking their cue from the teacher, they all agreed.

At the end of the day, when all the children had left, Teddy lingered, came over to her desk and said, 'Miss Thompson, all day long, you smelled just like my mother. And her bracelet, that's her bracelet, it looks real nice on you, too. I'm really glad you like my presents.' And when he left, she got down on her knees and buried her head in her hands and she begged God to forgive her.

The next day when the children came, she was a different teacher. She was a teacher with a heart. And she cared for all the children, but especially those who needed help. Especially Teddy. She tutored him and put herself out for him.

By the end of the year, Teddy had caught up with a lot of the children and was even ahead of some. Several years later, Jean Thompson got this note:

'Dear Miss Thompson: I'm graduating, and I'm second in my high school class. I wanted you to be the first to know. Love, Teddy.'

Four years later she got another note:

'Dear Miss Thompson: I just wanted you to be the first to know I'm graduating from college. The university has not been easy, but I love it. Love, Teddy Stollard.'

Four years later, there was another note:

'Dear Miss Thompson: As of today, I am Theodore J. Stollard, M.D. How about that? I wanted you to be the first to know. I'm going to be married in July. I want you to come and sit where my mother would have sat, because you're the only family I have. Dad died last year.'

And she went and she sat where his mother should have sat and she felt wonderful; because Teddy felt she deserved to be there. Then she remembered back ten years and wondered how things would have been different if she had not put on the perfume and bracelet."[19]

Frank's attitude to the story is so humane, so humble in its desire to treat all human beings equally, to give every individual that special chance. He says, "It occurs to me that with all the success we are having, it might be easy for us to somehow think we are better than someone else or to put people down because they look, act or speak differently (or even smell bad) or haven't experienced the success we have."

For Frank, success is not success unless it enables others; it is the true "power of one."

> "I hope that in our moment of celebrating our success, we will not pass up moments of putting on broken bracelets and old perfume."

"I doubt there is much true joy in being popular, keeping up with the Joneses or even getting ahead of the Joneses. But I believe there can be true joy in the kind of experience that Jean Thompson had when she sat where Teddy Stollard's mother would have sat."

His final words have a simple resonance that would have made his father proud of him, "I hope that in our moment of celebrating our success, we will not pass up moments of putting on broken bracelets and old perfume."[20]

And so, ever humble, ever thoughtful, Frank VanderSloot has demonstrated the message of "the power of one" in the way he has built Melaleuca itself. It has already touched hundreds of thousands of lives, customers and Marketing Executives alike. Frank built this principle into Melaleuca's marketing structure in such a way that each Melaleuca Marketing Executive is a single drop of water that when dropped into a still pond, sends ripples out to the furthest shores. It is "the power of one" multiplied a thousand-fold. It is the power that Frank, with all his humility and his solid values, has brought to a tremendous fruition. And it grows every day. How it grows is the subject of the next chapter.

CHAPTER 3

Redistributing the Opportunity for Wealth

A Look at Consumer Direct Marketing™

*"No army can withstand the strength
of an idea whose time has come."*

—Victor Hugo

 Come with me on a mental walk around a typical suburban neighborhood—perhaps like the one you live in. Walking down the street, we can see rows and rows of homes everywhere we look—hundreds and hundreds of homes. In each of those homes, there are pantries, shelves, and medicine chests full of products purchased at the local grocery store. In the bathroom you will find cabinets and counters full of hair care products, soaps, makeup, skin care products, and dozens of other personal-care items. You will find shaving cream, toothpaste, deodorant, pain relieving cream, first-aid items, and possibly vitamins. Perhaps under the bathroom sink you will find a selection of cleaning products. In the laundry room, or maybe under the kitchen sink, you will find dozens of bottles of household cleaners and laundry supplies.

It's basically the same story in every home we see. And in

most cases, the majority of products in these homes were manufactured by a handful of giant corporations like Procter & Gamble, Lever Brothers, and Colgate Palmolive.

Redistributing Opportunity — Competing Against the Corporate Giants

Unless you are a part of the supply chain for these products, there is probably no way you will ever share in the profits on the sales of these grocery store brands. These profits go into huge advertising budgets, to middlemen in the distribution chain, or to the grocery stores where the products are finally sold.

Melaleuca has made it possible for you to compete for customers against these manufacturers. Utilizing Melaleuca's marketing system, you can win customers away from these corporate giants one-by-one. Imagine customers up and down your street, and friends and family all over town, purchasing Melaleuca products from a catalog, and the profits going into your pocket, and the pockets of your friends, neighbors, and family members. This is what Melaleuca means by "redistributing opportunity"—taking the opportunity away from giant corporations and giving it back to families.

Utilizing Melaleuca's marketing system, you can win customers away from these corporate giants one-by-one.

This system of marketing has allowed American and Canadian families to compete against the "big guys"—and win. VanderSloot has stated that his goal is to have every household in America become a Melaleuca customer.

"We are going to take away their customers," VanderSloot states bluntly. "And we're taking tens of thousands of those customers each month. And we will learn to take more. And who will prosper? Not huge corporations, but American families."[1]

Consumer Direct Marketing™

There is an interesting anecdote about a new Melaleuca Marketing Executive who replaced all of the household cleaning products under her sink with Melaleuca's. The old products were laden with chemicals and potentially dangerous, as most traditional household products are. She decided to give away the old products to a neighbor instead of throwing them away. When the neighbor found out why she was giving them away, she was curious and began asking questions about Melaleuca products. The result was that she replaced her household products with Melaleuca's. She then added her old products to those of the first neighbor, then went to give them away to another neighbor.

No one has ever said what transpired after that, but time and imagination give rise to the image of a huge box of grocery store products being passed across America from family to family, growing larger all the time as they are replaced by Melaleuca products!

The story is not just whimsical; it's an apt illustration of the way Consumer Direct Marketing™ actually works. *Direct Marketing* is the process of marketing products through a catalog. But *Consumer Direct Marketing™* is very much like the process described in the anecdote. Each Melaleuca household buys only what they need each month from the catalog. If they then pass a catalog on to the next household, they will receive a commission each time that household buys from Melaleuca. Since everyone buys directly from Melaleuca, there is no need to carry an inventory, handle orders, deliver products or collect money. Melaleuca does all the work.

VanderSloot has stated that his goal is to have every household in America become a Melaleuca customer.

One of the most powerful aspects of Consumer Direct

Marketing™ is that your commissions are not limited to the households which you have personally introduced to Melaleuca. Should any of these households introduce other

"We have many Marketing Executives who receive commissions on thousands of customers who purchase Melaleuca products every month."

households to Melaleuca, you would receive a commission on *their* purchases as well. And this is true all the way through a possible seven generations of referrals. In other words, it's possible that, by introducing Melaleuca to only a dozen or so households, you could end up earning commissions on *hundreds* of households all over the country.

The commissions earned from each household can be rather small—only a few dollars each month. But the income is very steady and really adds up as more and more households learn about Melaleuca products.

"We have many Marketing Executives who receive commissions on thousands of customers who purchase Melaleuca products every month," says Frank VanderSloot. "And most of our customers never miss a month. That's because they love the products, and they can't purchase them anywhere else."[2]

The Origins of Consumer Direct Marketing™

As chronicled in Chapter 1, the original company, Oil of Melaleuca, Inc., opened for business in December, 1984. Roger and Allen Ball, and an Australian rancher, formed a partnership with the original idea to market products containing melaleuca oil. Early in 1985, they hired Frank VanderSloot to take over the management of the business. "We had several problems with that first business from the beginning," VanderSloot remembers. "And we closed it down five months after I came."[3]

Some of the problems VanderSloot mentioned stemmed from the system of marketing that the Ball brothers had chosen for the company, a system of marketing known as *multi-level marketing,* or *MLM.* As it turned out, the plan was illegal in all fifty states because it encouraged *inventory loading,* also known as *front-end loading.* VanderSloot could see that some of the company's distributors were getting hurt by this feature in the marketing plan. This experience made a deep impression on him. "Those were the most valuable five months of my business career," he says. "In those five months, I learned more about people, and their needs and feelings and hopes and dreams than I did in my entire business career or four years in college."[4]

When he and the Balls decided to start over again, VanderSloot, then an equal partner in the new venture, was determined to avoid the problems inherent with MLM systems. "At Melaleuca, we try to stay away from MLM concepts," he later said. "We believe that the hype and superficial excitement that surround these types of businesses is a deterrent to attracting intelligent, ethical people with a long-term perspective."[5] "We have been very careful not to build a company that looks like, smells like, or feels like multi-level ... Most multi-levelers have sold inventories, filled garages, and pestered their friends to the degree that they are now members of the 'NFL Club' (No Friends Left)."[6]

"We believe that the hype and superficial excitement that surround these types of businesses is a deterrent to attracting intelligent, ethical people with a long-term perspective."

The marketing system VanderSloot invented is totally unique. His idea was to combine the best elements of several different industries in such a way as to make operating a Melaleuca business simpler, and with less risk than other businesses. This had never been done before, partly because the technology needed had not yet been available. But advances which were occurring then in technology were making it possible. With VanderSloot's background in the data processing and communications industries, he recognized the new possibilities, and moved forward to invent a new system of marketing.

"I worked day and night," he remembers, "trying to develop a marketing plan that would give people a long-term opportunity to supplement their income, and to become financially independent."[7]

Melaleuca named this new marketing system Consumer Direct Marketing™. The reason it has been so successful is that it eliminates the extra work of handling products, payments, and deliveries, and allows the Marketing Executive to concentrate on activities that help his business grow, like enrolling new customers.

"We have found Melaleuca to be ten times easier and ten times better money!"

James and Mary Martha McCune testify to the simplicity of the Consumer Direct Marketing™ system. They had worked an Amway business for eight years, and finally quit when they realized they weren't going to make the money they were hoping to make. "Amway is a great company," says James, "but was way too much work for the money. We have found Melaleuca to be ten times easier and ten times better money! ... We've looked at a lot of other businesses and nothing compares to Melaleuca."[8] In only thirteen months they became Executive Directors with Melaleuca.

A member of Melaleuca's management team once put it in these words, "We realize that for someone to succeed in any business undertaking, one has to eliminate as many obstacles and distractions as possible. This is what Melaleuca has achieved."[9] VanderSloot accomplished this by examining the most efficient and most profitable businesses in the U.S. and adopting their best qualities. Here are some of the industries VanderSloot drew from and what exactly he took from each:

Consumer Products Industry

Melaleuca is part of the $90 billion consumer products industry, marketing over 100 consumable personal care, home care, pharmaceutical, and nutritional products, the same type of products every North American family already buys over and over again. These products are really the key to the marketing system's success. Without highly consumable products of exceptional quality, the system would not work. Melaleuca customers order the products month after month. In fact, over 95% of the customers who ordered last month will order again this month. This phenomenal re-order rate makes the concept of a stable residual income possible.

In fact, over 95% of the customers who ordered last month will order again this month.

VanderSloot once expressed the importance of the products in these words, "We don't have a right to be here unless we are marketing the best products for the best prices at the best value of anybody in this nation. And it's only when we develop that, and accomplish that, believe that, and do that, that we have the right to even have a business or to be in business."[10]

Direct Marketing/Catalog Sales Industry

The catalog sales industry has grown dramatically as people have less and less time to go out to shop for the things they need. Traditionally, direct marketing companies mail thousands of catalogs out to prospective customers, hoping they will buy from the catalog.

Marketing Executives share a catalog with friends, neighbors, and family members instead of the company mailing thousands

61

of catalogs to a bunch of faceless names. From then on the customer buys directly from Melaleuca by calling a toll-free number. Highly professional customer service representatives take the orders. And all orders are delivered directly to customers' homes via a special system involving private carriers and the U.S. Postal Service. This special system is designed to keep transit times short, costs low, and damage to packages minimal because they are handled less.

Direct Sales Industry

Direct sales is the type of sales that requires a face-to-face meeting with a prospective customer. Marketing Executives make a one-time presentation, explaining the product benefits and advantages, and then receive a commission on all future purchases made by the new customer. Depending on how well the Marketing Executive explains the advantages of Melaleuca products, he may have a loyal customer for life as a result of that one meeting.

Data Processing Industry

Melaleuca's data processing capability is what brings everything together to eliminate the extra work for the Marketing Executive. VanderSloot's background is rich with data processing experience. It was his knowledge in this area that led him to combine the various elements of the different industries together. This had never been done before. Probably because computer technology had not reached the level of sophistication to make it all possible. Today, Melaleuca has one of the most powerful computer systems and processes more data than most companies in the northwestern U.S.

In addition to order processing and tracking, payment collection, manufacturing and inventory functions, Melaleuca's computers do the monthly paperwork that, with other opportunities, would be handled by the home-based business owner. Each Marketing Executive in the company receives a computer-generated business report which details information needed to manage his business. This method of data processing provides accurate, efficient tracking of critical information, and gives the Marketing Executive more time to focus on activities which make his business grow. Simply put, instead of spending endless hours on paperwork, the Melaleuca Marketing Executive spends his time enrolling new customers, adding to his customer base and his income.

Simply put, instead of spending endless hours on paperwork, the Melaleuca Marketing Executive spends his time enrolling new customers, adding to his customer base and his income.

Insurance Industry

The elements already mentioned all combine to give the Marketing Executive the opportunity to earn *residual income*. This is a concept borrowed from the insurance industry, one of the most lucrative industries anywhere. The dictionary defines "residual" as "something left over." *Residual income* refers to income that is "left over" from something done in the past.

In the insurance industry, salesmen make a sales presentation one time. The customer then pays for the insurance on a monthly basis, and the salesman receives a portion of each payment for as long as the customer continues the policy. Instead of spending his time servicing existing accounts, the salesman spends his time selling more and more policies, increasing his residual income with each sale. VanderSloot says, "A good insurance salesman with a large clientele is set for life. The concept of residual income is powerful."[11]

To illustrate the contrast between Melaleuca and a company without the advantage of residual income, VanderSloot often uses the example of Avon. Avon is a multi-billion dollar company which has given women all over North America the opportunity to earn extra income. However, no matter how successful an Avon representative is in a given month, she will not earn a single penny the next month until she goes out and starts ringing doorbells again.

The only conclusion that one can draw comparing Avon to Melaleuca is that someday Melaleuca will also be a multi-billion dollar company. "When you consider the advantages of our product line and our residual income," states VanderSloot, "there is no comparison."[12]

Larry Pember echoes VanderSloot's sentiments. Having been a stock broker, Pember took a critical look at Melaleuca before getting involved. Residual income is a key reason for his success. "In the stock brokerage business, you are retailing. You are selling, but your production results in one month of income. The next month you're starting over," he explains. "Melaleuca is a business that produces residuals. As an example, a personal friend of mine was my second customer. That first month I believe I earned $14.00 from his purchases. Now, 22 months later, I earn approximately $1,000 a month from the sales in his organization. This is residual income!"[13]

When asked how much he made from his first month's work with Melaleuca, he typically replies, "I don't know yet. I'm still getting paid for it."

Another Executive Director puts it in a slightly different context. When asked how much he made from his first month's work with Melaleuca, he typically replies, "I don't know yet. I'm still getting paid for it."

The concept of residual income is somewhat difficult to fully comprehend. Most people are so accustomed to the traditional method of compensation—money in exchange for time—that they find it difficult to grasp exactly what a solid residual income could mean for them in their lives. Below is a situation that may help you understand what residual income could possibly mean to you and your family.

The Power of Residual Income

John is twelve years from retirement. In meeting with a financial advisor, John learns that his Social Security check will only cover a small part of the income he will need—assuming the Social Security system is still solvent when he retires. To have the lifestyle in retirement that he and his wife want, John will need to come up with an additional $40,000 per year on his own. His financial advisor tells John that he will need at least $400,000 in savings, before retiring, in order to draw $40,000 per year in interest, at 10%. To accumulate $400,000 John must invest $1,450 per month for the next 12 years at 10% interest.

John basically has two choices. He can work a second job to earn the $1,450 per month—the "traditional approach." Or he can develop a "residual income."

John basically has two choices. He can work a second job to earn the $1,450 per month—the "traditional approach." Or he can develop a "residual income."

Please note that these examples are simplified for the purpose of clarity. I have not taken into account inflation, tax ramifications, or various other factors. In estimating the time required to build a Melaleuca business, I have tried to be conservative, but, to use Melaleuca's verbiage, this information "is not necessarily representative of what any individual Marketing Executive will earn with this program."[14]

So, in considering our hypothetical example of John, the traditional method for increasing income would be through a part-time job. In that case, we see a picture something like this:

With his skills, John could figure on earning, after taxes, around $15.00 per hour at a part-time job. He will need to work about 96 hours per month, or about 22 hours per week at his part-time job to be able to invest the $1,450. With this approach, John will have to work about 13,824 hours over 12 years to fund his retirement.

If we consider the same situation with a Melaleuca business, it would work very differently. John could develop a residual income with Melaleuca that would not only accumulate a retirement fund, but continue to generate income through his retirement years. The actual logistics of John's situation might pan out something like this:

Hourly Comparison in John's Example

13,824 hours needed

1,040 hours needed

Residual   Traditional

Using the *Annual Income Statistics* sheet that Melaleuca provides, John can see that he needs to achieve at least the Director V level. According to Melaleuca, the average time it takes to reach this level is 17 months. After talking to several experienced Marketing Executives, John decides that this goal is attainable for him, but to be conservative, he decides to give himself 24 months as opposed to the average 17.

Instead of working 22 hours per week at a part-time job for the next 12 years, John will put in about 10 hours per week for the next *two* years building his Melaleuca business. John will focus on developing solid, product-centered customers and business builders so that his income will be stable throughout his retirement.

Let's compare the probable results of these two approaches:

"Traditional Income" Approach

John will have to work about 22 hours per week, part-time, for the next 12 years in order to be able to invest $1,450 per month. That's about 13,824 hours total. After 12 years, he will have accumulated about $400,000 in savings. At 10% interest, he can withdraw $40,000 per year without touching the principle. Added to what he expects to get from Social Security, John expects to be able to live comfortably, as long as he can get a good return on his money, and inflation stays at a reasonable level.

"Residual Income" Approach

John will work his Melaleuca business 10 hours per week for the next two years to build his residual income up to $1,450 per month. The total number of hours worked to achieve this level would be about 1,040—less than 1/13th the time using the traditional method. After two years, John will begin to invest $1,450 per month at 10% interest, and should accumulate $297,000 before his retirement date. At retirement, he should be able to withdraw $29,700 per year without touching the principle. This falls short of his $40,000 per year goal. But John would still have his $1,450 per month residual income—about $17,400 per year. Add the two incomes together, and John will earn $47,100 per year—or $7,100 per year more than his goal, not including his income from Social Security.

Even if John continued to work his Melaleuca business at 10 hours per week for the entire 12 year period, he would still be investing less than half the number of hours verses the traditional method. And, of course, he could build a much larger residual income with the extra time invested. Also, his Melaleuca business can be willed to someone else when John passes away.

How Solid is a Melaleuca Income?

Many other companies claim to offer a business opportunity with residual income. However, upon careful inspection, it is often found that these business opportunities have weaknesses that make this claim false.

Most home-based opportunities, especially MLMs, have a very low reorder rate and a very high dropout rate. According to *Kiplinger's* magazine, many MLM companies have dropout rates hitting 80% to 90% annually. In contrast, Melaleuca consistently has a 95% reorder rate. That is, 95% of the people who ordered last month will order again this month. This extremely high retention rate reflects the loyalty of Melaleuca customers and the popularity and consumability of the products.

"During the time that I was away, my business continued to grow because Melaleuca people continue to love the products."

With other opportunities, it takes a significant amount of time and effort just to maintain your income. And, with some of these, quite a bit of that time must be devoted to inventory management, taking orders, delivering product, accounting and other paperwork. After establishing one of these home-based businesses, some people find that they would be making more money and have fewer headaches had they just gone out and gotten a part-time job.

Another very important factor in a residual income opportunity is the effort required to enroll someone. With some of these businesses, it's very difficult to get anyone else involved.

68

According to Jim Head, who was formerly with a prominent MLM, "In that MLM, we had to give 100 presentations to get ten people to join. Out of that ten, seven would leave. Of the three left, one would make it to the equivalent of Director—*maybe*. In Melaleuca, eight or nine out of every ten people we present to enroll. Anyone who chooses to, becomes a Director. Now when someone *doesn't* enroll we're surprised. When we ask why, they usually say it's bad timing. But it's really because they think Melaleuca is too good to be true."[15]

I have heard or read about many other individuals within Melaleuca who consistently have this same kind of success. That doesn't mean that everyone does this well. But it does indicate the appeal of Melaleuca products and Consumer Direct Marketing™ as a business opportunity. Melaleuca's high enrollment and low drop-out rates are further proof of this appeal.

"A new 'deal' comes along every week. In fact, several dozen MLM companies start up every week, and just as many go out of business."

Another factor that very few people think about is the failure rate of the companies offering these opportunities. If you finally build your residual income up to the level you want, and the company goes out of business the next day, your income is gone. "A new 'deal' comes along every week," says VanderSloot. "In fact, several dozen MLM companies start up every week, and just as many go out of business. It breaks our hearts to see people we know and love go through these agonizing experiences."[16]

Melaleuca's focus has always been on "building a business to last a lifetime." With a thirteen year track record, no debt, and the highest possible Dun & Bradstreet credit rating, it certainly seems that they are serious about keeping this pledge.

Something else to look for—some opportunities have what

is called *breakaways*. We'll talk more about breakaways later in this chapter, but this basically means that when someone is successful in your organization, they may "break away" from your organization and take their sales volume with them. This could leave you scrambling to make up that volume just to maintain your current income level. In my opinion, any business opportunity with breakaways is not a true source of residual income.

Melaleuca does not allow breakaways. Once a customer is in your organization, they stay, no matter how large their organization becomes. This policy fosters a sense of cooperation and friendship among those in an organization. There is never any reason to be fearful of the success of anyone in your group.

"We don't want to be a multi-level company. We don't look like one. And we don't want to be thrown into the bucket that multi-levels are normally thrown into. The reason we don't want to be thrown into that bucket is because that bucket smells bad to a lot of people across America."

Nona Pione understands the soundness of Melaleuca's residual income. In 1994, she was diagnosed with cancer and pulled away from building her business for six months. "From the time I learned that I was ill, my focus turned from my business to my own care," she reflects. "This took all my time and direction away from my business. Had this been another company, my business would have been in shambles. But I was able to pick up from where I left off."

Now in complete health, Nona has a new outlook and a new appreciation for her residual income. "During the time that I was away," she says, "my business continued to grow because Melaleuca people continue to love the products. When I finished my treatment, I treated myself to a three week vacation in Europe. I don't know of any other business where one can do this—especially traditional businesses."[17]

Consumer Direct Marketing™ vs MLM

Because Melaleuca offers a home-based business opportunity, and it pays commissions on multiple generations of customers, it is sometimes mistaken as a multi-level marketing company. And, although some aspects of the Melaleuca business opportunity resemble a multi-level, the differences are, in reality, night and day.

"We don't want to be a multi-level company," VanderSloot says with conviction. "We don't look like one. And we don't want to be thrown into the bucket that multi-levels are normally thrown into. The reason we don't want to be thrown into that bucket is because that bucket smells bad to a lot of people across America. It smells bad because people have used multi-level marketing to hurt people. It smells bad because they've used it to scam people. They've used it to work shenanigans on people—to con them into money-making schemes. We have never done that. And we don't want to be associated with those kinds of businesses."[18]

VanderSloot's determination to keep Melaleuca out of that MLM "bucket," has taken some interesting turns at times.

VanderSloot's determination to keep Melaleuca out of that MLM "bucket," has taken some interesting turns at times. In 1995, *Success* magazine published a cover-story entitled "We Create Millionaires." Against VanderSloot's request, *Success* featured Melaleuca in that article, along with several multi-level companies. What's interesting about this incident is that those other companies were probably thrilled to be included. I can imagine the managers at the corporate offices of those other companies running around giving each other "high fives" upon learning that they were included. Being a company that "creates millionaires" would certainly give it some clout in terms of attracting business builders.

But VanderSloot's reaction was quite different. He said, "We wince because of some of the other companies we were thrown in with. Not because they are all bad people or bad companies, but because some have a bad reputation for creating bankruptcies as opposed to millionaires, and others have been tarnished by bad press and run-ins with state Attorneys General."[19]

Although Melaleuca is committed to keeping out of that MLM "bucket," the company is sometimes compared with companies in the MLM industry. One notable occasion in which Melaleuca was compared with some MLM companies was in its inclusion in the book *Multi-Level Marketing: The Definitive Guide to America's Top MLM Companies.* In that book, the authors did an analysis of each company's compensation plan to give readers a basis for comparison. According to the book's figures, Melaleuca has—by far—a more generous compensation plan than the top MLM companies did.

According to the book's figures, Melaleuca has, by far, a more generous compensation plan than the top MLM companies did.

This may explain why many people are coming to Melaleuca from MLM companies. VanderSloot states emphatically, "We welcome them, but ask that they do not bring their 'MLM' culture with them."[20] It may very well be that most of these people are coming to Melaleuca to escape the MLM culture, attracted by Melaleuca's honest approach and mission to enhance lives. However, it's interesting to note that most of the top Marketing Executives have no previous home-based business experience at all.

The Pitfalls of the MLM Culture

Many MLM people do come into Melaleuca after disappointing experiences. Of course, their initial reaction to Melaleuca is one of suspicion. After all, they've had their fingers burned once already. But it's an indication of the soundness of the Melaleuca opportunity that, not only do they get converts from people who have lost substantial amounts in an MLM, but that these people stay—and flourish.

Ed Bestoso, one of Melaleuca's top Marketing Executives is an example of this. He went bankrupt partly because of his MLM experience. But, having served his time in an MLM and lost everything, he was able to turn his life around again with Melaleuca.

With a history like Ed's, it was an odd experience when he received a phone call from an MLM marketer actually trying to convert him from Melaleuca to an MLM! The man had heard Ed was doing well with Melaleuca.

In fact, the guy was in real trouble—he'd quit a $60,000 a year job to take up the MLM scheme, upsetting his wife badly.

He obviously thought Ed would be a prime candidate for the MLM he was with. Ed realized very quickly that the man was very new to the game and totally unaware of what he was getting into. In fact, the guy was in real trouble—he'd quit a $60,000 a year job to take up the MLM scheme, upsetting his wife badly. What's more, he had invested over $33,000 into the business, $20,000 of which went into purchasing product—the kind of high-risk, front-end loading that Melaleuca shies away from. The guy had been given some training, but it cost him over $3,000.

One of the biggest problems with MLM-type businesses is *breakaways*—i.e., losing top people when their organization gets too big; a chief cause of the financial tragedies that befall MLM people.

73

Ed recalls the phone conversation: "I asked him if it was a 'breakaway' plan. 'What's that?' he replies. Then he tells me that he's never heard of 'breakaways,' so he guesses his company doesn't have them."

Ed realized the guy was in a real fix. But at the time, he thought he wouldn't be able to help the guy because he was obviously in too deep. Nevertheless, Ed told him enough about Melaleuca to "whet his appetite" and hung up, saddened by the experience.

Forty minutes later, the guy called back. Apparently the company *did* have a breakaway plan and the guy was very scared indeed. He asked Ed if he could help, so Ed arranged for him to come over to his house. There, they sat for hours, pouring over the two marketing plans, point by point, until one o'clock in the morning. "By the time he leaves," says Ed, "he's a different person. ... He is totally committed to Melaleuca. It turns out that we are exactly the kind of business he *thought* he was getting into."

"He is totally committed to Melaleuca. It turns out that we are exactly the kind of business he thought he was getting into."

Within four days, Ed's new-found friend had turned his life around. He had enrolled four Preferred Customers and one of them had enrolled three more. For Ed, there was the satisfaction of saving someone the pain and heartache that had led to his own bankruptcy. Ed muses, "I feel like I've given him back his values. I feel like I've helped to give his family a secure future. I guess I feel about as good as you can feel."[21]

Ed had, in fact, saved the man's entire future. And the main tools he had used to do so were simple facts, plain truth and a genuine concern for the man. Ed's concern for others is the primary reason for his tremendous success in Melaleuca.

You Don't Have to "Fake" It To "Make" It

There are several points I want to make about Ed's story. First, many MLMs are promoted by hype and deception. Ed's friend obviously had no idea what he was getting into. Why? Because the person who got him involved in the MLM didn't give him the whole truth. They obviously painted him a very rosy picture about quick riches and the good life. But it's clear that they didn't explain the marketing plan, and they didn't explain the risk involved.

Regarding the honesty issue, Melaleuca Corporate Director, Greg Lagana, said it best, "When I first talk to someone who's learned marketing in an MLM, I'm talking to someone who's been taught to 'fake it till they make it.' That means 'reality' and 'truth' must be avoided at all costs."[22]

In Melaleuca there's no reason to be misleading in any way. VanderSloot often holds up his father as an example to follow, "He was known as an honest man. I never heard my father tell a lie. He didn't exaggerate. He was the master of the understatement."[23] VanderSloot is constantly imploring people to deal honestly with others. "Let's make sure that we do not exaggerate the benefits of our products or the potential of our compensation plan," he says. "The truth is good enough! We should not expand on it!"[24] And, "We have nothing to hide."[25] To this end, Melaleuca has created an *Annual Income Statistics* sheet which very clearly shows how much Marketing Executives make at each level of achievement, the percentage of people who reach these levels, and the amount of time it took them to get there. No other company, that I know of, makes this information available.

"When I first talk to someone who's learned marketing in an MLM, I'm talking to someone who's been taught to 'fake it till they make it.' That means 'reality' and 'truth' must be avoided at all costs."

Don't Quit Your Job!

Another difference in Melaleuca is the emphasis on keeping your job. Ed Bestoso's friend quit his $60,000 a year job to work his MLM business. MLMers are trained that this is the way to succeed. They tell their distributors that if they won't quit their job, then they don't possess the desire needed to be successful. If

"We advocate that if you have a job, keep it! Be the absolute best employee you can be. Don't let anyone talk you into quitting your job to go full-time into Melaleuca. That usually does not make good sense."

he does quit his job, the result is that the MLMer has no choice but to make his business work. In desperation, he is tempted to use unethical practices to entice prospects to join him to help him build his business.

MLM guru, Mark Yarnell, author of the book *Power Multi-Level Marketing*, teaches this tenet of the MLM culture with these words: "You see, what you've got to do, if you're approaching this from an opportunity standpoint, is almost preposterous. It's almost so preposterous—it's such a tall order—most people couldn't do it. And that is, you're going to—in forty-five minutes, hopefully—cause a person to see the value in quitting his or her profession and going into network marketing (MLM)."[26]

Melaleuca's culture is—and has always been—don't quit your job. "Melaleuca's about adding to your current income—not replacing it," says VanderSloot.[27] "We advocate that if you have a job, keep it! Be the absolute best employee you can be. Don't let anyone talk you into quitting your job to go full-time into Melaleuca. That usually does not make good sense."[28]

Invest Your Time, Not Your Money

With regard to investing large sums of money, VanderSloot says, "To date, not a single person we know of has gotten hurt in any way by being involved with us. There is no inventory loading. In fact, there is absolutely no reason to carry an inventory or make any major investment whatsoever, other than one's time and energy."[29]

To anyone not familiar with MLM systems, an investment like $33,000 seems ridiculous, but unfortunately it is all too common. People will invest their life savings in the hopes of a big payoff.

Melaleuca's philosophy is, "If we treat the customer right and sell him a superior product at a good price he will buy again the following month and the next and the next," VanderSloot explains. "That means a steady stream of income month after month, year after year. The MLM companies don't seem to understand that philosophy. They want all their money *now* and they will do anything to get it— including seducing their customers into buying hundreds or thousands of dollars of inventory."[30] Melaleuca requires an investment of only $29—and even that is refundable. There is no risk with Melaleuca.

"If we treat the customer right and sell him a superior product at a good price he will buy again the following month and the next and the next."

Struggling With Conscience

Another anecdote which will help you to understand the MLM culture is from Jim Head. Jim and his wife, Lorena, have a background in the MLM industry. In fact, they left a troubled MLM company to enroll in Melaleuca. Jim remembers his experiences with that company, "With that MLM, we were always struggling to have the right 'posture,' to have conviction during recruitment presentations. Presentations always had to be done in a specific order—'A' before 'B,' 'B' before 'C,' 'C' before 'D'—

or it didn't make sense as a business opportunity. If you got 'D' before 'B,' you went bust every time. And we knew that only seven percent of what we communicated was the words. The rest was nonverbal, our body language. So there we were, worried about smiling at the right places, terrified we're going to get the parts out of order—trying to look relaxed and confident. But that wasn't *really* the reason we struggled. The real reason was conscience. We knew in our hearts that without the hype—without some vague promise of 'momentum' that was going to carry people to ridiculous levels of wealth—the whole thing made no sense at all.

"In Melaleuca," he continues, "suddenly we have 'posture' without even trying. Why? Because we're at peace with ourselves. We're not asking people to put their futures at risk. We're not holding up an unrealistic carrot. We're *telling* about Melaleuca, not selling it. We've given the Melaleuca presentation backwards, upside down, even when we had the flu—and people still enroll. Because Melaleuca makes perfect sense. We'd been enrolling for three weeks before it suddenly dawned on us that there is absolutely no reason to say 'no' to Melaleuca. There's no realistic objection, because there's nothing wrong with it, nothing hidden, nothing dishonest."[31]

"There's no realistic objection, because there's nothing wrong with it, nothing hidden, nothing dishonest."

Due Diligence Leads to Melaleuca

According to VanderSloot, about half of the Marketing Executives who reach the leadership level have no previous home-based business experience. However, some of Melaleuca's top Marketing Executives came from the MLM industry. In 1992, Tom Pisano, Nona and Rene Pione, and Ed Bestoso teamed up to investigate 48 different businesses. They had all previously been with MLM companies, and were looking for an opportunity that fit their "ideal" for a home-based business. They established ten criteria by which they could judge the companies. The criteria included things like no breakaways, high demand consumable products, good company track record, high quality management team, and so on. The only company that met all of the required criteria was Melaleuca. Then they spent seven weeks investigating the company. "We checked it out thoroughly," says Bestoso. "We liked the high reorder rate and the low attrition. But the best thing we saw was that no one was getting hurt, and there were lots of people making money." Bestoso, Pisano and the Piones are now high-level Executive Directors in the company. "It was the best thing we ever did," says Bestoso.[32]

Alan Pariser left his existing $6 million direct sales business to join Melaleuca. Before enrolling, he and his wife spent two full months researching the company. "We called the FDA, several Attorneys General, and a number of [Executive Directors]," says Alan. "We even flew to Idaho Falls to visit with Frank VanderSloot." They did all this because, as Alan explains, "We knew that whatever we did, it would ultimately affect our lives and thousands of other lives. We wanted it to be long-term and to bring others value. We saw that Melaleuca stood head and shoulders above everything else—and we had looked at 60-70 other programs. We knew that we could bring this business to anyone ... and we were totally impressed."[33]

"We knew that whatever we did, it would ultimately affect our lives and thousands of other lives. We saw that Melaleuca stood head and shoulders above everything else— and we had looked at 60-70 other programs."

Hundreds of thousands of people have now taken advantage of the opportunity to compete against the huge conglomerates that dominate the consumer products market. Melaleuca Marketing Executives are winning customers away from these giants by the tens of thousands each month. The company's unique market system is only part of the reason for this. Another important part is the company's product line. In the next chapter, we'll look at some of the products which have been key to Melaleuca's success, and the philosophy behind them. It's a simple philosophy with profound health implications. Melaleuca calls this philosophy the "Best of Science and Nature."

CHAPTER 4

The Best of Science and Nature

*"If a man has good corn or wood or boards or pigs to sell,
or can make better chairs or knives, crucibles or church organs
than anybody else, you will find a broad, hard-beaten road to
his house, though it be in the woods."*

—Ralph Waldo Emerson

 When Frank VanderSloot took over the original Oil of Melaleuca, Inc., it stumbled primarily over two factors—illegality and problems with the products, which had been formulated by inexperienced people. In an effort to avoid these problems with the new company, VanderSloot decided that Melaleuca's products must be "the best of science and nature"— in other words, natural products whose properties had been verified or improved scientifically.

Looking back, he says, "The marketing and delivery of exceptional products at reasonable prices has been the key to our success."[1] With this realization came the knowledge that public credibility was essential if Melaleuca was to continue with its successful expansion. Credibility was what Frank had in mind when he cautioned Marketing Executives about over-optimistic claims for product properties, "It is well known that our industry has, in the past, been plagued by fraudulent companies intent on making a fast buck and moving on. Too often, the individuals involved have only one thing in mind—to get rich quick, regardless of who gets hurt."[2]

Remembering his father's example, Frank repeatedly urges his Marketing Executives to understate any claims made about the products. Frank's caution is wise. The "natural health" movement has become a target for corporate business. Manufacturers with an eye for the market trends know that if they tout the "naturalness" of a product, it will sell to consumers who, suspicious of modern pharmaceuticals, will grab at anything deemed "natural."

Melaleuca will not release a product unless it is well documented and researched.

Thus, consumers are being flooded with a host of products designed to ride the wave of popularity for "natural" ingredients. Environmental concerns and the numerous side-effects which plague modern medicines are the subjects of a score of health-related magazines and TV programs. As a result, consumers are demanding safer, healthier, natural products. But the fact is, they don't always get them.

"Natural" doesn't always mean safe; nor does it always mean harmless. In fact, the word "natural" has no official definition at all when it comes to a product's ingredients. Practically anything can be advertised as "natural." And manufacturers sell these products with very little science or research behind them.

In contrast, Melaleuca will not release a product unless it is well documented and researched. The public has a tendency to snap up "natural" cures very quickly and there is a plethora of "holistic" products on the market that have not been adequately tested or whose claims have not been substantiated.

An example of this is melatonin. It hit the market a few

years ago and is now being sold openly in pharmacies and health stores across the country. Melatonin is an extremely complex hormone. It regulates sleep and sexual cycles in men and women; it regulates the body's clock in its day-to-day rhythms—and much, much more. It is a tremendously powerful hormone which interacts with other hormones in a complex manner little understood. In the U.K. and Europe it has been banned, and yet in America it is being sold by the jarful as a "sleep supplement"—which is rather like taking large doses of estrogen for something as mundane as pimples, and equally as foolish.

This is *not* the Melaleuca way. The entire line of Melaleuca products is safer, with minimal environmental impact and diligently-documented research. As Frank has put it, "No amount of wealth will bring true happiness if it is gained unethically."[3]

The Pioneer Product: Melaleuca Oil

When VanderSloot started up Melaleuca, Inc. with the aim of creating an exceptional product line, he needed a supply of melaleuca oil that would meet his quality standards. He went to great lengths to secure a crop which could propagate a superior tree line, for it was found that no two strains of the Melaleuca alternifolia tree provided the same quality of oil. His investigations took him to Australia. The best stands of Melaleuca alternifolia trees are in an area called the Bungawalbyn Reserve™. It was found that the Bungawalbyn varieties produced genetically-superior trees that gave the highest quality oil. The properties of the tree were so highly thought of by the local Aborigines that the very word Bungawalbyn means "healing ground." VanderSloot was able to secure exclusive

"No amount of wealth will bring true happiness if it is gained unethically."

rights to the oil harvested from natural stands of the Bungawalbyn trees which had never been treated with herbicides or pesticides.

Under Melaleuca's incentive, the growers actively sought out the more robust and higher-yield trees, took seedlings from them and began establishing plantations of trees from this superior line. The active and enthusiastic participation of the Australian growers was ensured by Melaleuca, who supported them through years of poor yields or bad crops—and the growers responded with a greater diligence in producing the highest-quality yield possible.

These pure oils have been shown to be superlative treatments for stings, burns, skin rashes and a host of topical applications.

As research on melaleuca oil progressed, it became obvious that the medicinal and soothing properties were directly proportional to the *grade* of oil. Higher grades of the oil have greater levels of the therapeutic agent Terpinen 4-ol and less of Cineole, which can be irritating to sensitive skin.

VanderSloot could see that some companies were selling sub-standard grades of the oil as "pure oil of Melaleuca alternifolia." Some of these oils have very little, if any, medicinal value. He wanted to make sure that Melaleuca sold only the highest-quality oil available, and that the customer could clearly see what grade they were getting. He decided to place the grade designation right on the label, and hence the name "T36-C7™" for the standard high-grade oil, and "T40-C5™" for the ultra-rare grade oil. These pure oils have been shown to be superlative treatments for stings, burns, skin rashes and a host of topical applications. Because the higher grade of the oil comes from trees with rare genetics and the supply is limited, it is more expensive.

Melaleuca recently raised the standards for both of their oils to "T36-C5™" and "T40-C3™," which demonstrates a commitment to making the very best oil available as growing and harvesting techniques continue to improve. The standard high-grade oil is used in a wide range of Melaleuca products, most notably in skin care, hair care, dental care and medicine chest products.

Even though reputable organizations the world over, including major Australian research foundations, have validated melaleuca oil's effectiveness and safety, VanderSloot is always cautious about its claims. By 1996, over six million bottles of the oil had been sold. Nevertheless, when describing its uses, Frank insisted on erring on the conservative side, "It's clear that melaleuca oil has some very unique and unusual properties. Many people have experimented and reported very favorable results on conditions such as cold sores, canker sores, candida, chicken pox, herpes, thrush, etc. Several studies have been done on some of these conditions that appear quite promising. But more research needs to be done to verify its efficacy before being able to make legitimate claims in regard to these conditions."[4]

The book is not yet closed on melaleuca oil. In some ways, it is still a mystery and, as of yet, not all of its properties are fully understood. New research is expanding its possibilities every day.

The book is not yet closed on melaleuca oil. In some ways, it is still a mystery and, as of yet, not all of its properties are fully understood. New research is expanding its possibilities every day. One thing can be said for certain—that as new uses are discovered for this wonderful substance, Melaleuca will ensure that any potential benefit is passed on to customers.

Beyond Melaleuca Oil

Nearly 30% of Melaleuca's revenues go into product quality. Compared to this, traditional manufacturers only spend about 10% for the same purpose. By pouring revenue back into product development, Melaleuca has been able to provide an ever-widening range of new products, many of which are not based on melaleuca oil at all.

Melaleuca's research and development team continually searches for natural ingredients with known restorative or curative powers. Having found such an ingredient, Melaleuca will either look closely at the validity of any former research conducted on it, or they will initiate new research. As a result of such investigations, Melaleuca now distributes a line of products which utilize ingredients that go far beyond the original flagship product, Melaleuca® oil. Nowadays, many of the products are not based on the oil at all, but on other natural botanicals—plants and herbs whose health-promoting properties have been known for years and whose validity has been established by further testing.

Having found such an ingredient, Melaleuca will either look closely at the validity of any former research conducted on it, or they will initiate new research.

A Safety and Health Issue

With heightened awareness of toxic substances at both the personal and environmental level, some consumers are beginning to actively question product safety. However, as a group, most are still very uninformed about the dangers residing in their very own homes in the form of cleaning and personal care products.

Large corporations have been more concerned about their own bottom lines than what is beneficial to the consumer. As such, the cleaning and personal care products distributed by industry giants are designed to maximize profit and not health concerns. The facts are staggering. The average home today contains more chemicals than were found in a typical chemistry laboratory at the turn of the century.[5] Cleaning products typically contain harmful chemicals like ammonia, chlorine, phenol and formaldehyde.

But cleaning products are not the only culprits. The Natural Institute of Occupational Safety and Health found that after analyzing 2,983 chemicals used in personal care products, 884 were found to be toxic.

The average home today contains more chemicals than were found in a typical chemistry laboratory at the turn of the century.

The analysis showed that of these, 778 can cause acute toxicity, 146 can cause tumors, 218 can cause reproductive complications, 314 can cause biological mutations and 376 can cause skin and eye irritations.[6]

It would seem that every household kitchen and bathroom is a minefield of hazards that is negotiated every day by families blissfully unaware—until something goes wrong. The most disturbing aspect of this is the possibility that children can come to grievous harm from these "everyday" products. Parents are only human and, despite their diligent supervision of drugs and over-the-counter medicines, they often forget that there is an array of poisons, even more lethal, just under the sink. Cleaning products are by far the most dangerous—window cleaners, bleaches, laundry detergents, to name just a few.

In 1994, the statistical Handbook for the American Family[7] showed that, of children aged 0 to 14 years, fifteen out of every one hundred thousand *dies* from poisoning every year. The figures for those who survived are much higher, and many of them suffered third-degree burns, loss of eyesight, a permanently damaged esophagus—and worse.

Even more insidious than these dramatic accidents is the "gradual" type of toxicity in which exposure over a length of time may bring about harmful diseases such as cancer, birth defects, ADD, asthma, liver damage or a compromised immune system. The chilling aspect of this is that often the original cause is never brought to light, so the problem persists.

As if that wasn't enough, every day, well-meaning homemakers, who don't realize the implications of their actions, pour gallons of toxic chemicals down the drain. The run-off from domestic waste water effects the rivers and oceans in ways far more complex than ever thought of before.

The practice of adding phosphates to detergents has always been an accepted policy by the giant soap corporations, regardless of the fact that the run-off has proven to be extremely harmful to the delicate balance of life in lakes, streams and rivers. Aerosol propellants in sprays have been directly linked to holes in the ozone layer, which are also responsible for an alarming rise in skin cancer.

Even more insidious than these dramatic accidents is the "gradual" type of toxicity in which exposure over a length of time may bring about harmful diseases such as cancer, birth defects, ADD, asthma, liver damage or a compromised immune system.

The list of household horrors is all the more striking because it is *absolutely unnecessary.* For almost every one of those household products which is highly dangerous, there's a Melaleuca equivalent which is safer, environmentally sensitive and of superior quality and performance. Dedicated to its mission of "enhancing the lives of those we touch," Melaleuca has expanded into a line of household products that follows the ancient biblical creed of "Hurt not the earth, neither the sea nor trees."[8]

Americans are slowly becoming aware that protecting the environment is not just the province of the fanatical few. The gap between the violation of nature's delicate balance and its rebound effect on humanity is growing narrower every year. Melaleuca has offered a solution where the giant corporations have simply turned a blind eye. This has created a competitive edge for the company as it attracts more and more people who realize they can now exercise environmental responsibility without sacrificing effectiveness.

Unlocking Nature's Secrets with Science

Early in Melaleuca's history, VanderSloot established relationships with a network of many scientists, researchers, universities and chemists who could help the company develop its products. As Melaleuca has expanded, there seems to be a peculiar sense of appropriateness in the direction taken by this developmental network. Following its establishment of safer, natural household products, Melaleuca's move into the area of nutrition and personal health aids seemed a natural step. "We have found that mother nature has provided a natural solution for almost every health problem that confronts us. Our task is to use science as the key to unlock the secrets that nature has to offer," states VanderSloot.[9]

"We have found that mother nature has provided a natural solution for almost every health problem that confronts us. Our task is to use science as the key to unlock the secrets that nature has to offer."

As Melaleuca R&D uncovers newer developments in natural health, the flexibility of their infrastructure facilitates their ability to investigate and incorporate such developments into an enhanced product line. This is accomplished on a time scale which would be impossible for the gigantic corporations. Not only does this put Melaleuca on the cutting edge, but the speed at which it takes place does not compromise safety or quality.

Fructose Compounding

Given some of the negative factors of modern life—stress, pollution, over-processed foods—it is even more essential that we ensure our body receives an adequate supply of vitamins and especially minerals. Sadly, a healthy diet which includes the recommended intake of fruits and vegetables does not always provide the necessary nutrition. If the minerals are not in the soil, they won't be reproduced in the food. Thus, the degeneration of soil quality and the practice of over-processing food has given rise to a peculiarly American phenomenon—people who over-eat and are still malnourished.

Sadly, a healthy diet which includes the recommended intake of fruits and vegetables does not always provide the necessary nutrition.

Given the strictness of FDA labeling on most foods, it is puzzling that there's no methodology to ensure that "fresh" fruits and vegetables actually do have the appropriate content of minerals and vitamins.

Nutritional research has also shown that even when there *is* an adequate mineral supply within a certain food, it doesn't necessarily mean that the body will receive its full benefit. This anomaly came to the attention of nutritionists in Egypt, Libya and Iran in the 70's, where children were suffering from horrible symptoms of zinc deficiency—severe growth retardation and dwarfism—even though the local foods contained an adequate supply of zinc.

The explanation is that the zinc attaches itself to certain acids in the food and is passed right through the body as "waste," without even getting to the cells. This happens, though to a lesser degree, with the minerals in *our* diets as well. The problem is solved by using an innovative process which binds the mineral to fructose, a substance found in fruit which is very readily absorbed by the cells. By using this "fruit sugar" messenger to carry the minerals piggy-back style, the mineral is passed through to the tissues and its full benefits can be utilized by the body.

This patented process, called "fructose compounding" is exclusive to Melaleuca. No one else has this cutting-edge technology, which is one of the features of Melaleuca's Vitality Pak™, a health product delivered to the customer's door in the shape of fifty-five vitamins and fructose-compounded minerals.

The Case of Bobbie McCaughey

Melaleuca's emphasis on using only those quality products which have been validated and well researched has had some interesting repercussions in the community at large. Not the least of these is the case of Bobbie McCaughey, the Iowa woman whose claim to fame is the delivery of seven living children at one birth.

Bobbie was carrying seven babies. So it was absolutely essential that she had the right nutrition.

When Bobbie had recovered from the news that she was pregnant seven times over (if, indeed, she ever did recover!), she was very concerned about nutrition. Her pastor's wife, Ginny Brown, is a Melaleuca Marketing Executive. Ginny suggested that Bobbie use the Vitality Pak™. Of course, Bobbie had to have her doctors look over the specifications of the Vitality Pak™. They examined the ingredients closely before approving them. Bobbie embarked upon a regimen of three Mel-Vita® and Mela-Cal® tablets, and three ProVex Plus™ capsules daily. The most distinctive advantage of the Vitality Pak™ is the high absorption of minerals which is due to Melaleuca's patented fructose-compounding process.

Bobbie says, "We thought it would be a great help during the pregnancy and that it would be much more usable—as far as being absorbed by my body—than a regular prenatal vitamin would be."[10]

A pregnant woman has very special nutritional needs. For instance, Bobbie was supposed to eat 4,000 calories a day, but she could not eat that much. "I needed to eat something every forty minutes and I just couldn't."[11]

Zinc and calcium are especially needed even during a normal pregnancy. In this case, the situation was even more extreme—Bobbie was carrying seven babies. So it was absolutely essential that she had the right nutrition. But, for the first five months of the pregnancy, she was so sick she could hardly eat at all. Once she got to the hospital she was able to eat a little bit more, but she says, "But then I had hospital food, so I didn't want to eat any more! So it was good to have something that was really able to boost the vitamins and minerals I didn't get from the food."[12]

Bobbie says, "We thought it would be a great help during the pregnancy and that it would be much more usable—as far as being absorbed by my body— than a regular prenatal vitamin would be."

The circumstances of a pregnancy seven-times over needed very special precautions—and Bobbie was told by her doctors to stay in bed for the last five months of the pregnancy. This immediately introduced other possible problems—blood clotting in the legs, reduced muscle tone, and loss of bone mass. Also, a common aspect of multiple pregnancies is that blood pressure can rapidly escalate to abnormal proportions. The doctors who had examined the ingredients of the Vitality Pak™ told Bobbie to take three Mela-Cal® and three Mel-Vita® tablets every day—and she never had any problems with blood pressure.

Ginny, knowing that it might be difficult for the McCaughey's to pay for the vitamins in such quantities, called Tish Poling in the president's office and Tish discreetly arranged that the McCaughey's would get everything they needed from Melaleuca—without any intrusive publicity.

When Bobbie was asked how she felt during this period, she replied, "I felt really good. It wasn't until probably the last week and a half that I really felt terrible. By that time, the contractions had started and I was on other medications to stop them."[13]

Of course, Frank VanderSloot was proud that Melaleuca's vitamins and minerals had been used in such a medically-sensitive situation. He said, "We're really pleased that the McCaugheys decided to use our vitamins, and that the result has been so great. Our hopes and prayers are with them as they prepare for the wonderful experiences ahead."[14]

"We're really pleased that the McCaugheys decided to use our vitamins, and that the result has been so great. Our hopes and prayers are with them as they prepare for the wonderful experiences ahead."

Well, the results have become world-wide news. Bobbie did deliver her seven bouncing bundles of joy—the first woman in history to do so. Naturally, the credit should go to her and her team of doctors. Still, there is no doubt that Melaleuca's policy of credible testing and high-quality product meant that the Vitality Pak™ was well up to their standards.

A comic side-light to the Bobbie McCaughey case took place during one of Frank VanderSloot's talks. While addressing a roomful of people, Frank mentioned that Bobbie had been taking the Vitality Pak.

"All of a sudden," Frank said, "from the back of the room, a woman screamed, 'OH MY GOSH!!' It seems she was a new customer and she'd just started taking the Vitality Pak™ herself. She was concerned that somehow that was what caused the seven babies!"[15]

Vitality For Life™ Program

Melaleuca launched the Vitality For Life™ program in 1993. A fitting tribute to Melaleuca's dedication to total health, Vitality For Life™ is an unprecedented effort to deal with health care at its very roots. It's a medical fact that most degenerative diseases in America stem from lifestyle choices, including diet and exercise. The chief weapons that Melaleuca uses in its fight to eradicate ill-health are *nutrition* and *knowledge*.

The knowledge required is furnished by the Wellness Assessment Program. The program employs trained counselors and an established network of medical professionals to help customers identify their personal health concerns. The counselors also provide continued support and advice, enabling the customer to initiate and maintain lifestyle changes to supplement other nutritional and health measures.

It's a medical fact that most degenerative diseases in America stem from lifestyle choices, including diet and exercise.

In establishing the Vitality For Life™ program, lifestyle and nutrition were of paramount importance. Most ill health in America stems from stress, toxins and an unhealthy lifestyle. The leading cause of death is heart attacks. Over a third of adults and adolescents are obese and 50% have excessive body fat, which is directly linked to heart attacks and strokes caused by high blood pressure and "bad" cholesterol. Cancer is the next leading cause of death, accounting for one out of each five deaths in the United States.

In light of these statistics, this statement from Sir McFarlane Burnett, who won the Nobel Prize for immunology, is a major revelation: "Over one thousand cells become cancerous in the body each day, but if the immune system is functioning normally, it destroys these cancer cells."

The fact is, the body is capable of dealing with a disease as radical as cancer if the immune system is functioning normally. But factors such as poor nutrition, lack of exercise, obesity and toxins impair the body's immune system so that its defenses are easily breached. With this knowledge as its foundation, the Vitality for Life™ program deals with these concerns on an individual basis, and attempts to address those factors which render the individual prone to disease.

The Access® Bar

Exercise is a key element in a healthy lifestyle. Obesity is a major concern, and lack of exercise is a main contributor to strokes and heart attacks. The Access® Bar was developed specially to ensure that the maximum possible benefits were obtained from exercise.

Through Melaleuca's practice of networking with cutting-edge doctors and scientists, they became aware of Dr. Lawrence Wang's studies into fat metabolism.

Through Melaleuca's practice of networking with cutting-edge doctors and scientists, they became aware of Dr. Lawrence Wang's studies into fat metabolism. Dr. Wang, Ph.D., is the Professor of Animal and Human Physiology at the University of Alberta, Edmonton, Canada, and a member of the prestigious Royal Society of Canada.

His research into fat metabolism led him to a substance called *adenosine* which exerts a blocking effect on the burning of stored fat during exercise. Adenosine, a by-product of activity,

95

leads to the familiar sensation in fatigued muscles, expressed in the old exercise slogan as "feel the burn." It is adenosine which is indirectly responsible for that burning sensation, and muscle soreness after exercise. Normally, exercise burns off glucose, not fat, but by utilizing a natural substance which inhibits the effect of the adenosine, Wang was able to increase the direct burning of fat and *not* glucose during exercise.

This led to the Access® Fat-Conversion Activity Bar, a product made from natural substances which has become a mainstay for both athletes and casual exercisers alike. Taken approximately fifteen minutes before exercise, the bar ensures that the body will burn less glucose and more fat. Fatigue and soreness are minimized and exercise can continue for longer periods. This simple, safe exercise bar ensures that maximum benefits can be attained during any exercise routine.

In 1995, Melaleuca initiated a research program whose results are so astounding that they may achieve nothing less than the complete transformation of the way doctors deal with America's number one killer— heart disease.

Melaleuca's interest in formidable health issues did not stop with obesity. In 1995, Melaleuca initiated a research program whose results are so astounding that they may achieve nothing less than the complete transformation of the way doctors deal with America's number one killer—heart disease.

The Evolution of ProVexCV™

In 1995, Melaleuca announced that they were committed to becoming a world leader in research and development into a group of substances known as flavonoids. This was in direct response to the enormous medical problem of heart disease and the related medical and lifestyle factors associated with it.

The results have been quite amazing, leading VanderSloot to remark, "We never dreamed that when we said we would become a world leader, we would actually become *the* world leader in the development of products to reduce the risk of heart disease."[16]

Melaleuca's interest in flavonoids had been aroused by a peculiar phenomenon known as the French Paradox which came to the attention of the public in 1990. The way in which the story develops is a prime example of Melaleuca's product development methodology.

Apparently, the French consume 2.8 times the amount of lard as Americans and 3.8 times as much butter. The French are also a nation of very heavy smokers. Yet, despite the fact that they have higher blood cholesterol levels and higher blood pressure readings than Americans, the French have only one-third the rate of heart attacks.

"We never dreamed that when we said we would become a world leader, we would actually become the world leader in the development of products to reduce the risk of heart disease."

Subsequent research led scientists to attribute this odd paradox to the French's habitual consumption of red wine with meals. This led to further studies into the constituents of red wine, aimed at pinpointing the connection between the wine and their lowered incidence of heart attacks. Over the years, many such experiments gradually eliminated different factors until, finally, something concrete was established. It seems the lowered incidence of heart attacks in the French was due to a substance in grape skins and seeds known as flavonoids. Flavonoids are present in red wine and purple grape juice.

The basic causes of heart attacks had already been well established by earlier researchers. It stems from two factors—

97

the buildup of "oxidized" cholesterol on artery walls, which causes the artery to become restricted; and the "stickiness" of blood platelets which may cause a blockage in the restricted artery.

The buildup of "bad" cholesterol has been shown to be minimized by anti-oxidants such as Vitamin E; and also, as early as 1974, it was demonstrated that aspirin can reduce artery blockage by inhibiting platelet clotting.

This simplified explanation indicates that any attempt to reduce heart attacks has to be a two-fold attack—one, to produce an anti-oxidant that reduces the oxidation of "bad" cholesterol; and two, to reduce blood platelet "stickiness" in a similar manner to the action of aspirin.

Dr. Folts says, "Focusing on flavonoid supplements was the next logical step. Everyone has been asking when they'll be able to get the same benefits [of red wine] from a pill."

Aspirin has one major drawback. Most heart attacks are induced through stress, and it was found that aspirin's effect is minimized in the presence of adrenaline, which is released during stress—the "Catch 22" of using aspirin for this purpose.

Melaleuca, in typical response to the challenge of a new area for research, formed an alliance with Dr. John Folts, the man who had conducted the original research into the beneficial effects of aspirin. Folts had already spent several years researching the effects of flavonoids on platelet stickiness. He believes that flavonoids are the key to the "French paradox." Folts says, "Focusing on flavonoid supplements was the next logical step. Everyone has been asking when they'll be able to get the same benefits [of red wine] from a pill."[17]

Melaleuca's goal was to develop a flavonoid-based dietary supplement that would be effective at preventing heart disease.

The initial research indicated that flavonoids extracted from plants are not absorbed completely by the body. This was very disappointing news at first.

Other manufacturers of flavonoid supplements were touting them as being beneficial for heart disease prevention based on tests which were done in test tubes only. Melaleuca's research had been done in living subjects and clearly showed that the claims made by the other manufacturers were greatly exaggerated.

The researchers set out to solve the problem of absorption so the benefits of the flavonoids could be utilized by the body. After almost two years the researchers discovered that a particular mixture of flavonoid extracts combined with a special blend of enzymes greatly increased the absorption of the flavonoids. This was the breakthrough they had been looking for. This breakthrough led to the development of the first flavonoid-based supplement which has been proven (in living subjects) to be effective in curbing the two primary causes of heart disease.

After almost two years the researchers discovered that a particular mixture of flavonoid extracts combined with a special blend of enzymes greatly increased the absorption of the flavonoids. This was the breakthrough they had been looking for.

"When the Truth is Almost Too Good to Be True"

This was the title of Frank VanderSloot's September 1997 President's Message, which is a direct response to the results of Dr. Folts' research. The results, to put it mildly, have been over-whelming. A ripple of excitement fluttered through the Melaleuca world as the breakthrough product, known as ProVex*CV*™, was made available to Melaleuca Marketing Executives at the 1997 Convention. The staggering implications of this and the excitement it has aroused will be discussed in more detail in our next chapter.

Frank VanderSloot, however, in accordance with long-established Melaleuca principles, is asking for calm and restraint. Though it is apparent a major breakthrough has been made, he urges Melaleuca Marketing Executives to refrain from any publicity until Dr. Folts and his researchers can publish their findings in appropriate medical journals.

Where it will take Melaleuca is, as of yet, an untold story with unlimited possibilities.

Melaleuca's success in promoting the research on flavonoids is not a lucky accident. By casting its search net wide, Melaleuca is ever sifting through the enormous number of natural substances that can yield remedies to all kinds of illnesses.

"We did exactly that with ProVex™—instead of becoming a competitor or follower in that industry, we found a better way, and we became the leader."

The larger corporations simply will not take time to investigate natural remedies, for one reason—they cannot be patented. And smaller companies simply don't have the funds to pursue the kind of research that led to ProVex*CV*™. So Melaleuca has carved out a huge niche for itself in the marketplace as the leading manufacturer of beneficial natural products.

In networking with scientists, university researchers and doctors, Melaleuca ensures it stays at the forefront of scientific knowledge. As a result, Melaleuca is able to oust any competitor by improving on a product, such that the Melaleuca version will always be the very best available on the market.

In his February 1997 address, Frank VanderSloot emphasizes this, "If any company, large or small, comes out with a great product, rather than competing with it, we'll incorporate it into our own product line—and we will challenge our own scientists to improve on it. We did exactly that with ProVex™—instead of becoming a competitor or follower in that industry, we found a better way, and we became the leader."[18]

Melaleuca, Inc.'s expansion and success has always been inextricably interwoven with the quality of its products. Astute choices in research and uncompromising testing have borne fruit in more ways than one. In the words of Frank VanderSloot, "As our ongoing research continues to uncover more of nature's secrets, we promise to keep you informed. We believe this is a never-ending story, but the first chapter is now complete ... Stay tuned for more information."[19]

That information and its implications paint a picture for Melaleuca which in not just rosy but absolutely astounding, as presented in our next and final chapter, *What the Future Holds*.

CHAPTER 5

What the Future Holds

"The best way to predict the future is to invent it."

—Alan Kay

"If we build Melaleuca using correct principles, fifty years from now, Melaleuca will be even a better opportunity than it is today."[1]

—Frank L. VanderSloot

Back in the days when the new-born Melaleuca, Inc. was taking its first hesitant steps, no one could have predicted just how successful the company would become. There are signs that even back then Frank VanderSloot's plans were to build something gigantic, something new, something that would alter the face of the American consumer market.

When he left his stable, high-paying job at Cox Communications to join forces with the Ball brothers, it seemed like a very radical move. His colleagues at Cox Communications obviously thought so, too. There is a story about Frank's farewell party at Cox in which they bedecked a tree with tea bags. (Frank had told them about the "tea tree" and "tea tree oil.") It was a joke, but the kernel of truth was that Frank's colleagues obviously thought this was a wild leap into the dark. With the 20/20 vision of hindsight, it now seems that, in fact, it was a leap of faith.

VanderSloot took another leap of faith after the old Oil of Melaleuca, Inc. failed miserably.

Why, we must ask, would a reputable businessman respond to the total failure of a business by drawing out his life savings and plunging back in again as Frank did? The answer is that this was the opportunity that Frank had been looking for all his adult years—to build a business based on the principles at the core of his own value system. Frank has often urged his Marketing Executives to "act on your dreams." Frank, himself, acted on his own dream. He was convinced even back then that here was an opportunity to build a thriving business on the principles he'd learned at his father's knee.

In 1994, Frank waxed nostalgic about the company's origins, saying, "It has been nine years since we launched Melaleuca Inc., on September 1, 1985. I remember wondering what the future would bring and who would join us as we began to build the company. I was convinced that there was a great opportunity for us to impact people's lives in a very positive way."[2]

"I remember wondering what the future would bring and who would join us as we began to build the company. I was convinced that there was a great opportunity for us to impact people's lives in a very positive way."

This was Frank's personal dream. Since then, the wheel of time has turned, and that future is now the present, and Melaleuca has succeeded beyond even Frank's wildest dreams. Frank speculated in the beginning that there would be some individuals who would build their annual income to one or two hundred thousand dollars. As it stands today, there are several families who are earning nearly one million dollars a year.

Melaleuca income was, of course, always meant to be supplemental, a point which Frank always emphasized. "We advocate that if you have a job, keep it!"³ The present situation is that checks are sent out to over 150,000 families per month and often the "supplemental" income is far in excess of the income a family receives from full-time employment.

The analogy Frank has drawn here is that of the benchmark results used in modern athletics. Often a line is drawn as the pinnacle of achievement in athletic performance. Then, as soon as someone exceeds this benchmark, others follow suit—and the level is raised even further. As was the case with the four-minute mile. "No one had been able to run a mile in less than four minutes; now there are hundreds, maybe thousands of disciplined athletes who run faster than that during routine workouts."⁴

What had once been seen as impossible has now become commonplace. If we apply this analogy to Melaleuca, the pinnacle benchmark was that of Corporate Director. People shook their heads—"no way; it's impossible." Then the first person achieved that "impossible status"—Russell Paley—at the tender age of 26. This was followed shortly by Gregory and Sherry Lagana and then Kim Smith. Three in a row for an achievement once deemed impossible. The best estimates are that all of these Corporate Directors will earn over a million dollars in 1998.

People shook their heads. "No way; it's impossible." Then the first person achieved that "impossible status," Russell Paley, at the tender age of 26.

The growth of Melaleuca has been staggering and the transformation of the Marketing Executives' earning capabilities has been paralleled by the transformation in the product line. It began with Melaleuca® oil-based products, and now, new products and health care systems exist in abundance. Despite this change, the basic principles of Melaleuca have never changed.

They are the same plain truths established more than a decade before by an ex-Idaho farm boy with bedrock-solid convictions. It is these truths that have enabled Melaleuca to attain its present success and the same "plain truths" will steer it into the next century and beyond.

"In the beginning we were so excited about this phenomenal melaleuca oil that we expected our entire product line to revolve around melaleuca oil. We had no idea then that there were dozens of other natural ingredients that would be even more exciting and even more beneficial, but in different ways.

"We just had a phenomenal product called melaleuca oil, and we wanted to enhance lives."

"We did not anticipate the power of fructose compounding, or the impact of proanthocyanidins. We had not learned of Dr. Wang's research on adenosine inhibitors, all the advantages of complex carbohydrates, or the benefits of glucosamine. We had not learned of 'moisture magnets' or the potency of antioxidants. We just had a phenomenal product called melaleuca oil, and we wanted to enhance lives."[5]

A phenomenal product and the desire to enhance lives is a stirring reminder that these were the twin pillars on which Melaleuca was built and, as we turn our focus to the future, these sturdy pillars continue to support Melaleuca. Frank built a business to last a lifetime—not his lifetime but everybody's. What VanderSloot has provided is a structure which protects and sustains a flame which, like the Olympic torch, will never go out. Melaleuca has changed, and the world around us is changing, yet VanderSloot firmly believes that no matter what changes science may bring, there are certain basic values that will never change. "Regardless of all the truths science unveils, we will continue to value these things that are deepest in our hearts ...

things like relationships, caring, trust, honor and decency ... a sense of community, of family, and of being and doing good."[6]

His system works. The proof is in the pudding. And now, Melaleuca is the best low-investment business opportunity of the last decade and it is not likely to lose this position as the new millennium begins.

VanderSloot's personal desire is that, without him, Melaleuca should maintain its lead right through the next one hundred years. "Of course, someone will have to take over after we are gone, but we are confident *The founding principles are unshakable, and Melaleuca is moving from pinnacle to pinnacle of achievement.* that there are those who will be ready when the time comes."[7]

The founding principles are unshakable, and Melaleuca is moving from pinnacle to pinnacle of achievement.

No doubt when Frank lets go of the reins the business will not just carry on, but it will actually flourish—it was made to do that.

New Breakthroughs, Unlimited Possibilities

To say Frank is happy with the future is something of an understatement. In his speech at the May 1998 Launch, as he described the potential of the new product, ProVexCV™, Frank was positively bubbling with excitement. The funding for this research has only been possible because of Melaleuca's financial success. Because of its policy of plowing profits back into research and product enhancement, Melaleuca has made a major breakthrough that could revolutionize heart disease prevention. Added to this, the sales from this new development could produce a quantum leap in Melaleuca's finances such that it could quickly become a billion dollar company. The potential for the future is positively unlimited.

Melaleuca is ever sensitive to natural products that have

potential therapeutic use. Thus, the excitement about grape seed extract as a possible treatment for cardiac problems caught their interest and they initiated a phase of research. Their aim was to become the world leader in the use of bioflavonoids and proanthocyanidins in the prevention of heart disease. Three years have passed since that research was initiated.

Melaleuca hired a prominent researcher to prove the value of grape seed extract in the prevention of heart disease in living subjects. Many of the claims made by other companies were based on test tube studies. The research found that these claims were largely false. Initially, this was bad news for Melaleuca. The hopes were that a natural remedy would be produced from these substances which could be added to Melaleuca's product line. In the end, however, this problem has actually turned out to be an enormous blessing.

In his Launch speech, he was so enthusiastic it was apparent that the testing was in and that something great was on the horizon.

The real potential of bioflavonoids as a treatment turned out to lie in a unique blend of enzymes discovered by, and exclusive to, Melaleuca itself. This new product has the power to reduce bad (LDL) cholesterol oxidation and blood platelet activity, the two main causes of heart disease. Thus far, cholesterol and platelet buildup have been treated by either Vitamin E and aspirin or pharmaceutically-prescribed medicines.

It is not customary for Frank VanderSloot to release news of a product before all the final testing is in, but in his Launch speech, he was so enthusiastic it was apparent that the testing *was* in and that something great was on the horizon. The only reason for his caution in avoiding publicity was his respect for the scientists' need to publish their account in the appropriate medical journals. He was absolutely adamant that the research had been successful.

Evolution of a Billion Dollar Product

At the same time as urging caution about revealing the findings to the press, VanderSloot was quite clear in depicting the facts, their validity and the implications for every Marketing Executive. These are the facts:

On September 26, 1997, Dr. John Folts presented the findings of his research on ProVex*CV*™ at the Midwest meeting of the American Federation for Medical Research. This reported the results of testing on dogs.

On May 2, 1998, Dr. Folts presented the findings from his research on ProVex*CV*™ to about one thousand researchers and scientists at the symposium BioMedicine 98 in Washington, D.C. This symposium was a report on the *updated* version of ProVex*CV*™ as tested on twenty dogs and twelve humans, including Dr. Folts himself.

Of these findings, Frank reports:

"We can tell you that the results of both the animal studies and the human studies are extremely exciting."

"We have learned more about grape seed, grape skin, bilberry and Ginkgo Biloba extracts and which specific ingredients do what ... We have also learned some exciting things about the most effective way to extract the nutrients from grape *"We have learned exactly how to do it and we are not telling anyone else. And much of what we know is now protected by patent."* seeds and grape skins ... We have learned exactly how to do it and we are not telling anyone else. And much of what we know is now protected by patent."[8]

Perhaps the most exciting aspect of these breakthrough discoveries is that the resulting product can be held exclusive to Melaleuca—in other words, no other company will be able to sell it. Apparently there is only one company in the whole of the

United States which knows how to implement the special process needed to get the maximum results from the grapes. Melaleuca has contracted with this company to have a special factory built. This factory will manufacture this grape extract utilizing the special process, exclusively for Melaleuca. Also, Melaleuca has taken out a contract with this manufacturer such that the contractor can only supply this special extract to Melaleuca for the next twenty years—i.e., Melaleuca has a monopoly.

"They will try to take this opportunity from us. But we will protect your right to prosper from this opportunity."

This astounding situation is an odd echo of the early days of Oil of Melaleuca, Inc. when an enthusiastic Frank VanderSloot thought he had a world monopoly on melaleuca oil—with a few crucial differences. In this case, the monopoly really exists. Melaleuca, still a small company, is entering a billion-dollar arena—a David against billion-dollar Goliaths. Prescription heart medicine costs a patient $7 a day and is a source of massive revenues for these pharmaceutical moguls. They will obviously put up a fight, especially as they are being ousted by a small company whose sales are made through ordinary people with home-based businesses.

Frank VanderSloot is ready for that. He is adamant Melaleuca will win. He says, "They will try to take this opportunity from us. But we will protect your right to prosper from this opportunity."[9] And he means it. This is a sincere, heartfelt promise to all his Melaleuca Marketing Executives.

The current market for such a product is staggering. What's more, the latest test results show ProVexCV™ to be not only better than Vitamin E and aspirin, the two leading over-the-counter products for combating heart disease, but even better than prescription medicines.

WHAT THE FUTURE HOLDS

The figures reveal it all: In America alone, every twenty seconds somebody has a heart attack; every sixty seconds, someone dies of a heart attack. And the number of people at high-risk for a heart attack is growing as the Baby Boomers hit middle-age.

The reason for Frank's jubilation is obvious. Melaleuca stands poised on the edge of an enormous leap into a huge captive market with a product that can combat the leading cause of death in the U.S. and Canada. To illustrate the potential of this product, VanderSloot uses the example of a promising new treatment for cancer, the number *two* killer.

Four years into the development of this new cancer drug, the press got hold of the story. It was the leading item on several news programs and a front-page article in several major newspapers. Even though this drug was more than a year from being tested in humans, and several years from being available to the public, the company's stock rose 330% the day after the news stories hit. This indicates the enormous potential for this product. However, there is no guarantee it will work in humans.

> *"I do not know of any company, regardless of size—let alone a Direct Marketing company—that has had the opportunity to take a product of this magnitude to market."*

VanderSloot compares this situation with the position that Melaleuca is now in. "We have the solution to the number one killer in North America. And we know that it works in humans,"[10] says VanderSloot. "I do not know of *any* company, regardless of size—let alone a Direct Marketing company—that has had the opportunity to take a product of this magnitude to market. It's so fun for me to think about! A product that is so far advanced beyond anything else in the marketplace! ... It's wonderful to be in a position where the truth is almost too good to be true. Thank goodness it *is* true. I cannot imagine a better situation for us to be in."[11]

Well, perhaps it would be difficult to imagine Melaleuca being in a better situation, but its potential does not stop there. Melaleuca's unique approach, its marketing system, its relationship-based sales and its value-based methodology are now being touted as the keys to business success. This information comes not from any Melaleuca public-relations team, but is the independent opinion of some of America's top business consultants.

> *"It's wonderful to be in a position where the truth is almost too good to be true. Thank goodness it is true. I cannot imagine a better situation for us to be in."*

A Bright Future—Trends from the Experts

Charles Handy has been described as a philosopher for the world of business and management. In his book, *The Age of Unreason*, he foresaw the collapse of the forty-five year job and the paternalistic company. American CEO's await with bated breath for his predictions. The first one is Handy's dismissal of the unscrupulous treatment of employees. He states that unless current companies find better ways of rewarding employees, they won't even make it into the second millennium—the companies will collapse through ill-will and inefficiency. "Corporate downsizing is leaving workers and managers burned out and lacking in values," he says.[12]

Handy also has pointed to ethics and lack of values as being the downfall of large corporations—he states quite bluntly that in allowing unscrupulous methods, lowered quality of product and unfair treatment of employees, such corporations are sowing the seeds of their own destruction.

"The old-fashioned models of corporate control and

contracts of employment are meaningless. Organizations have to be based on trust."[13]

Handy sees the present population of Baby Boomers as being the driving force of the future, particularly with their environmental awareness and their need for quality products. "They'll be the main consumers and the bulk of the voters. They'll spend more money on information, food, wine, books, CDRoms. They'll want smaller, quieter cars that pollute less. They'll care more about the environment, health, beauty, learning and less about consuming."[14]

Who, then, shall provide these "new consumers" with products of quality, sensitive to the environment? These experts all agree on one thing—the type of organization which will do this and survive the new economy has to be built on relationships, not profit. They point to the example of the "family-based" organizations of Italy and South China as the solution.

If these independent consultants had been trying, they could not have given a better description of Melaleuca. Yet they never intended to—they were simply referring to organizations in general which were the models of success for the new millennium.

"The power of capitalism will undoubtedly diminish unless we give more power to the real assets—people. If you want a model for the new sort of capitalism, you are more likely to find it in the family business networks in Italy or South China than in America or Germany. Like all extended families, these businesses are based on informal ties of mutual obligation. They move fast and they are prepared to sacrifice short-term profit for long-term benefits, and they know they are bonded to a common future."[15]

The same point has been made by Peter Drucker, one of the most perceptive observers of the American business scene. In

Forbes Magazine, March 1997, Drucker stated, "The kind of organization [that will succeed] will be built around family and regional ties that, unlike American business, are personal rather than impersonal."[16]

If these independent consultants had been trying, they could not have given a better description of Melaleuca. Yet they never intended to—they were simply referring to organizations in general which were the models of success for the new millennium. It is obvious how closely Melaleuca's structure fits their description.

Given their predictions, the demonstrable success of Melaleuca so far, and the fact that it has developed a new product with a billion-dollar potential, Melaleuca's future does look rosy. More than that—its future looks incredible.

Frank VanderSloot is quick to deflect personal praise back onto his Marketing Executives. Yet, it is apparent that it was his vision and his self-effacing leadership that has made Melaleuca what it is today—and what it can be in the future.

"I would call on all our people—customers, Marketing Executives and employees alike—to call themselves into action, to be good examples, to lead out in a good cause, to go to work and build dreams."

It is an awe-inspiring thought, given the Frank of today, that he was once rated as lacking in leadership skills. He has become a truly great leader; someone whose primary concern is not for himself but the people he leads. There are those who admire his leadership so much that they wonder what will become of Melaleuca when he finally goes. Frank responds by reminding them of the men and women—his mother and father foremost—who have influenced him, and points to this as an assurance of the continuity of Melaleuca without him. "The impact of these leaders is immeasurable because their influence continues to cause people to grow long after that influence has been exercised."[17]

The success of Melaleuca does not stem from its great structure, its incredible marketing plan or any of these factors alone. It is the values which have sustained it and the values that drive it. It was never just a job; it was, and still is, a cause. The purpose of Melaleuca is "to enhance the lives of those we touch," a theme that has been repeated throughout this book. By following this basic credo, Melaleuca has risen to heights previously believed impossible—and it will surpass its own accomplishments in the year 2000 and beyond. It is built on solid principles and it will last many lifetimes.

It is fitting to finish this book with the quiet words of Frank VanderSloot himself:

"There are many great causes in North America. I feel Melaleuca is a great cause. As our mission of enhancing the lives of others rolls forth, I would call on all our people—customers, Marketing Executives and employees alike—to call themselves into action, to be good examples, to lead out in a good cause, to go to work and build dreams."[18]

Sources

Introduction

1. Frank L. VanderSloot, "A Conversation with Frank L. VanderSloot," *Get Rolling* (video), Melaleuca, Inc., 1992.
2. "Frank L. VanderSloot Appointed to Board of Directors for U.S. Chamber of Commerce," *Leadership in Action*, Melaleuca, Inc., April, 1998: 5.

Chapter 1

1. Frank L. VanderSloot, "A Conversation with Frank L. VanderSloot," *Get Rolling* (video), Melaleuca, Inc., 1992.
2. *Body and Soul Magazine*, Dec., 1992.
3. Frank L. VanderSloot, *Why Melaleuca?* (audio), Melaleuca, Inc., 1998.
4. Frank L. VanderSloot, "A Conversation with Frank L. VanderSloot," *Get Rolling* (video), Melaleuca, Inc., 1992.
5. Frank L. VanderSloot, "President's Message," *Melaleuca Country*, Dec., 1997: 2.
6. Frank L. VanderSloot, "Building a Business to Last a Lifetime," *Business Enhancement Series Tapes - Vol. 36* (audio), Melaleuca, Inc., 1992.
7. Frank L. VanderSloot, "President's Message - We Must Police Ourselves," *The Melagram*, Melaleuca, Inc., Sept., 1991: 3.
8. Rob & Sherri Dias, *The Diamond Stories* (audio), Melaleuca, Inc., 1992.
9. "1991 Hall of Fame Inductees Honored," *The Melagram*, Melaleuca, Inc., Oct., 1991: 7.
10. "1991 Hall of Fame Inductees Honored," *The Melagram*, Melaleuca, Inc., Oct., 1991: 7.
11. Ron & Camille Frasure, *The Diamond Stories* (audio), Melaleuca, Inc., 1991.
12. *Nation's Business*, May, 1991.
13. *Inc. Magazine*, Oct., 1993.

Chapter 2

1. Frank L. VanderSloot, "President's Message - The Power of One," *Melaleuca Country*, Melaleuca, Inc., Sept., 1996: 3.
2. Frank L. VanderSloot, "Concluding Address from Melaleuca's Annual Convention," *Business Enhancement Series Tapes - Vol. 57*, Melaleuca, Inc., 1994.
3. Frank L. VanderSloot, "President's Message - The Power of One," *Melaleuca Country*, Melaleuca, Inc., Sept., 1996: 2.

4. Frank L. VanderSloot, "President's Message - The Power of One," *Melaleuca Country*, Melaleuca, Inc., Sept. 1996: 2.
5. Frank L. VanderSloot, "President's Message - The Power of One," *Melaleuca Country*, Melaleuca, Inc., Sept., 1996: 2.
6. Frank L. VanderSloot, "President's Message," *Melaleuca Country*, Melaleuca, Inc., Dec., 1997: 2.
7. Frank L. VanderSloot, "Concluding Address from Melaleuca's Annual Convention," *Business Enhancement Series Tapes - Vol. 57*, Melaleuca, Inc., 1994.
8. Frank L. VanderSloot, "President's Message," *Melaleuca Country*, Melaleuca, Inc., Dec., 1997: 2.
9. Francine Shapiro, PhD., & Margot Silk Forrest, *EMDR, The Breakthrough Therapy For Overcoming Anxiety, Stress and Trauma*, Basic Books, 1997.
10. Frank L. VanderSloot, "Concluding Address from Melaleuca's Annual Convention," *Business Enhancement Series Tapes - Vol. 57*, Melaleuca, Inc., 1994.
11. Frank L. VanderSloot, "Concluding Address from Melaleuca's Annual Convention," *Business Enhancement Series Tapes - Vol. 57*, Melaleuca, Inc., 1994.
12. Frank L. VanderSloot, "Concluding Address from Melaleuca's Annual Convention," *Business Enhancement Series Tapes - Vol. 57*, Melaleuca, Inc., 1994.
13. Frank L. VanderSloot, "Concluding Address from Melaleuca's Annual Convention," *Business Enhancement Series Tapes - Vol. 57*, Melaleuca, Inc., 1994.
14. Frank L. VanderSloot, "Concluding Address from Melaleuca's Annual Convention," *Business Enhancement Series Tapes - Vol. 57*, Melaleuca, Inc., 1994.
15. Frank L. VanderSloot, "Concluding Address from Melaleuca's Annual Convention," *Business Enhancement Series Tapes - Vol. 57*, Melaleuca, Inc., 1994.
16. Frank L. VanderSloot, "President's Message - This Thanksgiving Season," *Melaleuca Country*, Melaleuca, Inc., Nov., 1996: 3.
17. Frank L. VanderSloot, "President's Message - This Thanksgiving Season," *Melaleuca Country*, Melaleuca, Inc., Nov., 1996: 3.
18. Frank L. VanderSloot, "President's Message - This Thanksgiving Season," *Melaleuca Country*, Melaleuca, Inc., Nov., 1996: 3.
19. Frank L. VanderSloot, "President's Message - The Lives We Touch," *Leadership in Action*, Melaleuca, Inc., May 1996: 2.
20. Frank L. VanderSloot, "President's Message - The Lives We Touch," *Leadership in Action*, Melaleuca, Inc., May 1996: 2.

Chapter 3

1. Frank L. VanderSloot, "Building a Business to Last a Lifetime," *Business Enhancement Series Tapes - Vol. 36*, Melaleuca, Inc., 1992.
2. Frank L. VanderSloot, *Why Melaleuca?* (audio), Melaleuca, Inc., 1998.
3. Frank L. VanderSloot, *Why Melaleuca?* (audio), Melaleuca, Inc., 1998.
4. Frank L. VanderSloot, *Why Melaleuca?* (audio), Melaleuca, Inc., 1998.
5. Frank L. VanderSloot, *Why Melaleuca?* (audio), Melaleuca, Inc., 1998.
6. Frank L. VanderSloot, "President's Message - *Success* is Not What We Wanted," *Leadership in Action*, Jan., 1996: 2.
7. Frank L. VanderSloot, *Why Melaleuca?* (audio), Melaleuca, Inc., 1998.
8. *Leadership in Action*, Melaleuca, Inc., July, 1994: 4.
9. "Consumer Direct Marketing - A Revolutionary Idea Changing How North America Shops!," *Leadership in Action*, Mar., 1996: 22.
10. Frank L. VanderSloot, "A Conversation with Frank L. VanderSloot," *Get Rolling* (video), Melaleuca, Inc., 1992.
11. Frank L. VanderSloot, *Why Melaleuca?* (audio), Melaleuca, Inc., 1998.
12. Frank L. VanderSloot, *Why Melaleuca?* (audio), Melaleuca, Inc., 1998.
13. *Leadership In Action*, Melaleuca, Inc., June, 1994: 3.
14. *The Melaleuca Profile*, Melaleuca, Inc., Rev. 11/97.
15. *Leadership in Action*, Melaleuca, Inc., Dec., 1994: 4.
16. Frank L. VanderSloot, *Why Melaleuca?* (audio), Melaleuca, Inc., 1998.
17. *Leadership in Action*, Melaleuca, Inc., Aug., 1995: 3.
18. Frank L. VanderSloot, "Introducing: Consumer Direct Marketing," *Business Development Launch Highlights*, Melaleuca, Inc., 1993.
19. Frank L. VanderSloot, "President's Message - *Success* is Not What We Wanted," *Leadership in Action*, Jan., 1996: 2.
20. Frank L. VanderSloot, "President's Message - A Legitimate Business to Last a Lifetime," *The Melagram*, Melaleuca, Inc., Nov., 1992: 2.
21. *Leadership in Action*, Melaleuca, Inc., Nov., 1994: 4.
22. *Leadership in Action*, Melaleuca, Inc., Oct., 1994: 3.
23. Frank L. VanderSloot, "President's Message- The Power of One," *Melaleuca Country*, Melaleuca, Inc., Sept., 1996: 2.
24. Frank L. VanderSloot, "President's Message - Building with Correct Principles," *Leadership in Action*, Melaleuca, Inc., Apr, 1996: 2.
25. Frank L. VanderSloot, "Building a Business to Last a Lifetime," *Business Enhancement Series Tapes - Vol. 36*, Melaleuca, Inc., 1992.
26. *Mark Yarnell on MLM* (audio), MYD Publications, Inc., 1990.
27. Frank L. VanderSloot, "Introducing: Consumer Direct Marketing," *Business Development Launch Highlights*, Melaleuca, Inc., 1993.
28. Frank L. VanderSloot, "President's Message - Prospering in Difficult Times," *The Melagram*, Melaleuca, Inc., Feb., 1992: 2.

29. Frank L.VanderSloot, "President's Message - Building with Correct Principles," *Leadership in Action*, Melaleuca, Inc., Apr., 1996: 2.
30. Frank L. VanderSloot, "President's Message - A Legitimate Business to Last a Lifetime," *The Melagram*, Melaleuca, Inc., Nov., 1992: 2.
31. *Leadership in Action*, Melaleuca, Inc., Dec., 1994: 4.
32. *The Melagram*, Melaleuca, Inc., Aug. 1992: 3.
33. *The Melagram*, Melaleuca, Inc., Aug. 1992: 3.

Chapter 4

1. Frank L. VanderSloot, "President's Message - We Must Police Ourselves," *The Melagram*, Melaleuca, Inc., Sept., 1991: 2.
2. Frank L. VanderSloot, "President's Message - We Must Police Ourselves," *The Melagram*, Melaleuca, Inc., Sept., 1991: 2.
3. Frank L. VanderSloot, "President's Message - We Must Police Ourselves," *The Melagram*, Melaleuca, Inc., Sept., 1991: 2.
4. "Over Six Million Bottles Sold! ... of Oil That Is!," *Leadership In Action*, Melaleuca, Inc., Jan., 1996: 19.
5. Debra Lynn Dadd, *The Nontoxic Home & Office*, Jeremy P. Tarcher, 1992.
6. Judith Berns, "The Cosmetic Cover-up," *Human Ecologist* : 43 (Fall 1989).
7. Statistical Handbook for the American Family
8. Revelation 7:3, from "Hurt Not the Earth, Neither the Sea Nor Trees," *Melagram*, Melaleuca, Inc., Jan., 1995: 8.
9. "Over Six Million Bottles Sold! ... of Oil That Is!," *Leadership In Action*, Melaleuca, Inc., Jan., 1996: 19.
10. "... And Babies Make 10!," *Melaleuca Country*, Melaleuca, Inc., Feb., 1998: 17.
11. "... And Babies Make 10!," *Melaleuca Country*, Melaleuca, Inc., Feb., 1998: 17.
12. "... And Babies Make 10!," *Melaleuca Country*, Melaleuca, Inc., Feb., 1998: 17.
13. "... And Babies Make 10!," *Melaleuca Country*, Melaleuca, Inc., Feb., 1998: 17.
14. "... And Babies Make 10!," *Melaleuca Country*, Melaleuca, Inc., Feb., 1998: 17.
15. "... And Babies Make 10!," *Melaleuca Country*, Melaleuca, Inc., Feb., 1998: 17.
16. Frank L. VanderSloot, "President's Message - Proanthocyanidins: Attacking Heart Disease from Both Directions," *Melaleuca Country*, Melaleuca, Inc., Aug. 1, 1997: 2.
17. "Heart-Healthy Benefits of Wine, Grape Juice Now in a Supplement; Early Study Shows Flavonoid Supplement Prevents Blood Clot Formation," *PR News Internet Article*, May 13, 1998.
18. Frank VanderSloot, "President's Message - Leaping Ahead!," *Melaleuca Country*, Melaleuca, Inc., Feb., 97: 2.
19. Frank L. VanderSloot, "President's Message - Proanthocyanidins: Attacking Heart Disease from Both Directions," *Melaleuca Country*, Melaleuca, Inc., Aug. 1, 1997: 2.

Chapter 5

1. Frank L. VanderSloot, "President's Message - Building with Correct Principles," *Leadership in Action*, Melaleuca, Inc., Apr., 1996: 2.

2. Frank L. VanderSloot, "President's Message - New Opportunities Coming Our Way," *Leadership in Action*, Melaleuca, Inc., Sept., 1994: 2.

3. Frank L. VanderSloot, "President's Message - Prospering in Difficult Times," *The Melagram*, Melaleuca, Inc., Feb., 1992: 2.

4. Frank L. VanderSloot, "President's Message - A Great Year Ahead, A Great Year Past," *Melaleuca Country*, Melaleuca, Inc., Jan., 1997: 2.

5. Frank L. VanderSloot, "President's Message - More Excitement On Our Journey," *Melaleuca Country*, Melaleuca, Inc., Mar., 1997: 2.

6. Frank L. VanderSloot, "President's Message - It's More Than Just Winning," *Melaleuca Country*, Melaleuca, Inc., Apr., 1997: 2.

7. Frank L. VanderSloot, "President's Message - It's More Than Just Winning," *Melaleuca Country*, Melaleuca, Inc., Apr., 1997: 3.

8. Frank L. VanderSloot, *Address at May Business Launch*, May 1998.

9. Frank L. VanderSloot, *Address at May Business Launch*, May 1998.

10. Frank L. VanderSloot, *Address at May Business Launch*, May 1998.

11. Frank L. VanderSloot, "President's Message - When The Truth Is Almost Too Good To Be True," *Melaleuca Country*, Melaleuca, Inc., Sept., 1997: 3.

12. Carla Rapoport, "Charles Handy Sees the Future," *Fortune*, Oct. 1994: 155+.

13. Carla Rapoport, "Charles Handy Sees the Future," *Fortune*, Oct. 1994: 155+.

14. Carla Rapoport, "Charles Handy Sees the Future," *Fortune*, Oct. 1994: 155+.

15. Carla Rapoport, "Charles Handy Sees the Future," *Fortune*, Oct. 1994: 155+.

16. Robert Lezner & Stephen S. Johnson, "Seeing Things as They Really Are," *Forbes*. Mar., 1997: 122-128.

17. Frank L. VanderSloot, "President's Message - Leadership: A Powerful Concept," *Melaleuca Country*, Melaleuca, Inc., Nov., 1997: 3.

18. Frank L. VanderSloot, "President's Message - Leadership: A Powerful Concept," *Melaleuca Country*, Melaleuca, Inc., Nov., 1997: 3.